The Audiovisual Services Sector in the GATS Negotiations

The Audiovisual Services Sector in the GATS Negotiations

Patrick A. Messerlin, Stephen E. Siwek, and Emmanuel Cocq

The AEI Press

Publisher for the American Enterprise Institute
WASHINGTON, D.C.

and

Groupe d'Economie Mondiale de Sciences Po
PARIS

Available in the United States from the AEI Press, c/o Client Distribution Services, 193 Edwards Drive, Jackson, TN 38301. To order, call toll free: 1-800-343-4499. Distributed outside the United States by arrangement with Eurospan, 3 Henrietta Street, London WC2E 8LU, England.

The Groupe d'Economie Mondiale de Sciences Po (GEM) is an independent research unit which aims to improve the performance of French and European public policies in a global world and to promote debates on current and future globalization—its real magnitude and scope, its foreseeable consequences, the opportunities it offers and the obstacles to be overcome. GEM's work covers the full range of microeconomic policies related to globalization: it deals not only with the usual topics of international economic relations such as trade and investment policies, but also with topics related to competition and industrial policies, as well as to regulatory reforms in services.

For further information please visit http://gem.sciences-po.fr, or contact gem@sciences-po.fr.

Library of Congress Cataloging-in-Publication Data

Messerlin, Patrick A.
    The audiovisual services sector in the GATS negotiations/Patrick A. Messerlin, Stephen E. Siwek, Emmanuel Cocq.
        p. cm.
    ISBN 0-8447-7172-4
    1. Tariff on audio-visual materials. 2. Audio-visual materials—Government policy. 3. General Agreement on Trade in Services (1994) I. Siwek, Stephen E. II. Cocq, Emmanuel. III. Title.

    HF2651.A79A27 2003
    382'.457914—dc22

                                                            2003063554

Printed in the United States of America
10 09 08 07 06 05 04   1 2 3 4 5

Table of Contents

Tables

Foreword

In advanced industrial economies, the service sector accounts for a large portion of each nation's gross domestic product. Despite the increasing importance of services trade, the multilateral trading system began establishing rules to open markets in those sectors only in 1995, with the creation of the General Agreement on Trade in Services (GATS) at the conclusion of the Uruguay Round of trade negotiations. Decisions at the end of the round did provide for continuing negotiations in the services area. Only with the renewed commitment to a new round of trade negotiations, undertaken in November 2001 at the World Trade Organization (WTO) ministerial meetings in Doha, Qatar, however, did serious individual sectoral negotiations go into high gear.

The American Enterprise Institute is engaged in a research project to focus on the latest round of trade negotiations on services. The project, mounted in conjunction with the Kennedy School of Government at Harvard, the Brookings Institution, and the U.S. Coalition of Service Industries, entails detailed analyses of individual economic sectors: financial services, accounting, insurance, energy, air transport—and now audiovisual and entertainment services. Each study identifies major barriers to trade liberalization in the sector under scrutiny and assesses policy options for trade negotiators and interested private-sector executives. This audiovisual services study is being copublished with the Groupe d'Economie Mondiale de Sciences Po, a Paris research institute headed by Patrick Messerlin, one of the coauthors of the study.

AEI would like to acknowledge the following donors for their generous support of the trade-in-services project: American Express Company, American International Group (AIG), CIGNA Corporation, FedEx Corporation, Mastercard International, the Motion Picture Association of America, and the Mark Twain Institute. I emphasize, however, that the conclusions and recommendations of the individual studies are solely those of the authors.

CLAUDE BARFIELD
American Enterprise Institute
for Public Policy Research

1

Introduction

Audiovisual Services are at the heart of globalization, and at the same time they are important carriers of individual cultures.
—United Nations Conference on Trade and Development[1]

The audiovisual services sector has changed significantly during the past ten years. New technologies have stimulated the growth and development of audiovisual services and products around the globe and offer consumers worldwide access to a multitude of entertainment and information services. As part of the explosion in information technology that has taken place in the past decade, audiovisual services have played a role in fostering many nations' economic development, both through spreading information and ideas and by promoting investment in the advanced communications infrastructure of these nations. Electronically delivered audiovisual products and services that increase the use of this infrastructure are helping to create an environment that will encourage investment in the digital networks of tomorrow.

Globalization and new technologies also have implications for the amount of content available within a particular country. As services such as cable television, video-on-demand, and direct satellite broadcasts expand across borders, there is a need for content to fill the increasing number of broadcast hours they supply. Although viewers generally prefer local programs, if local programming is not available, it is inevitable that broadcasters will depend on imported programs to fill airtime. (Note that local and domestic programming are not the same thing. However, imported programs can be substitutes for both local and domestic programs.) In particular, the dependence of subscription broadcasting on foreign content is likely to remain high in the foreseeable future.

The United States is in a strong position to benefit from the increasing demand to fill broadcast hours. In some countries, certain policymakers fear that the overwhelming amount of U.S. products threatens cultural diversity and will eventually homogenize the world's cultures. To many people,

1

"globalization means the Americanization of the world and the subjugation of local cultures by the commercialism of Hollywood."[2] However, it is possible that those countries that recognize the strategic importance of fostering strong creative industries can enhance their own cultural resilience and benefit from globalization by encouraging the diversity that it promises.

Defining the Audiovisual Services Sector

In general, the audiovisual services sector covers a wide range of activities related to the production, distribution, and exhibition of audiovisual content such as motion pictures, radio and television programs, and sound recordings. In the General Agreement on Trade in Services (GATS) of the World Trade Organization (WTO), audiovisual services are defined under the subsector of communication services.[3] The GATS is the first and only set of multilateral rules and commitments covering government measures that affect trade in services. It covers all services, with two exceptions: services provided in the exercise of governmental authority and, in the air transport sector, air traffic rights and all services directly related to the exercise of traffic rights. Table 1 illustrates the subcategories of the audiovisual sector in the WTO in detail (and their associated listing under the United Nations Provisional Central Product Classification [CPC]).

However, there is growing uncertainty about the very notion of audiovisual services and their categorization within the context of new technologies. The United States has questioned the GATS classification of audiovisual services under communication services, objecting that it does not cover certain services, such as exhibition of films, operation of cinemas, and direct-to-home satellite services.[4] Moreover, many of these subcategories may be too vague or too narrow with digitization and convergence—which provide the potential for many kinds of digital content to be distributed over the same networks—and the emergence of new electronic media. For example, radio and, to a certain extent, television programs can be "streamed" over the Internet, and this type of broadcast will be greatly increased by broadband networks. More and more services may therefore be regarded as falling within the category "Others." With digital radio and television services enhanced by interactive and multimedia features, it will no longer be possible to draw a clear distinction between audiovisual services distributed through traditional broadcasting networks and those distributed online Consequently a case

TABLE 1
AUDIOVISUAL SERVICES AND THEIR SUBCATEGORIES IN THE GATS

Category with subcategories

CPC 9611	Motion picture and videotape production and distribution services	
	CPC 96111	Promotion or advertising services
	CPC 96112	Motion picture or videotape production services
	CPC 96113	Motion picture or videotape distribution services
	CPC 96114	Other services in connection with motion picture and videotape production and distribution
CPC 9612	Motion picture projection service	
	CPC 96121	Motion picture projection services
	CPC 96122	Videotape projection services
CPC 9613	Radio and television services[a]	
	CPC 96131	Radio services
	CPC 96132	Television services
	CPC 96133	Combined program making and broadcasting services
CPC 7524	Radio, television, and transmission services	
	CPC 75241	Television broadcast transmission services
	CPC 75242	Radio broadcast transmission services
CPC n.a.	Sound recording	
No CPC specified	Others (e.g., the contents of multimedia products)	

SOURCE: World Trade Organization, *Audiovisual Services*, Background Note by the Secretariat, S/C/W/40 (Geneva, 1998), 1–2. As modified by authors.
a. Especially for the subcategory radio and television services, it sometimes is difficult to determine the exact boundary between services classified under telecommunications and those classified under audiovisual services.

can be made for clarifying the current subdivisions. However, the main category "audiovisual services" has the advantage of not being linked to any particular form of technology. It is open for new technological developments and will thus stand the test of time.

Market Access Control in the Audiovisual Services Sector

Measures used by countries to protect the sector from the international market include content regulations, foreign ownership and control restrictions, and tax incentives and government subsidies. These measures aim to promote and enhance national culture. They are usually underpinned by the preference within a country for domestically produced programming.

Content Regulations. Content regulations, especially for television, are an important part of cultural policy in many countries. They can ensure that local programs, as expressions of a country's unique cultural identity, have a place on television and are accessible to the community. Content regulations can also foster the development of domestic production industries, which create local programs. Local content regulations for television typically restrict how much and at what times foreign programming can be shown by broadcasters by prescribing a certain percentage of local programming within the total amount of broadcast time. In addition, some countries have explicit requirements regarding the language used in programs broadcast on television and radio.

Foreign Ownership and Control Restrictions. Many countries prohibit foreign ownership and limit foreign investment in broadcast media, especially in television. They do this to ensure that their citizens have control over broadcasting services. These restrictions reflect concerns about cultural dominance by foreign interests and the need to safeguard and support domestic cultural industries. It is argued that reserving ownership for a country's nationals will tend to facilitate local expertise in broadcasting, with local owners more likely to employ local staff. This in turn is said to contribute to the development of a local creative infrastructure and the representation of local views in the media.

Tax Incentives and Government Subsidies. Population size and wealth can limit the extent to which local producers are able to recoup production costs in their domestic markets. Government assistance in the form of tax incentives and subsidies goes some way in addressing the limited capacity of domestic markets to support the development and production of film and television products.

The Audiovisual Services Sector in the Uruguay Round

The Uruguay Round of Multilateral Trade Negotiations concluded in April 1994 and resulted in the GATS. The negotiation of the GATS was the first time that trade in services, including audiovisual services, was brought within the ambit of multilateral trade rules. As discussed previously, the GATS covers the entire range of audiovisual services. The framework of the GATS—made by various countries to liberalize their current restrictions on trade in services—is divided according to four modes of supply. These modes describe how services are delivered into markets, and countries make commitments to remove (or maintain) trade-limiting regulations against them.

During the Uruguay Round negotiations on services, GATS concepts were reviewed in terms of their applicability to audiovisual services. At that time, strong disagreement emerged concerning the proposal to introduce a "cultural exception" into the Agreement. The negotiations between the United States and the European Community (EC) about the audiovisual services sector were one of the key remaining differences preventing a settlement on services. EC[5] member states, particularly France, and other countries, including Canada, India, and Australia, were opposed to U.S. demands for liberalized trade in audiovisual services. The United States argued that movies and television programs were commercial products just like any other. The United States contended that the EC's local content rules for television, which provide that a majority of transmission time is reserved for European works, unfairly imposed a market access barrier to U.S. audiovisual products and cost U.S. producers potential export income. The United States and other countries, including Japan, pressured the EC to commit to dismantling the local content rules.

The EC proposed a sectoral annex on audiovisual services aimed at ensuring that WTO members would maintain their right to differentiate among audiovisual products on the basis of their origin, that is, a derogation from the most favored nation (MFN) principle. The annex would have allowed for quantitative limitations (for example, screen time) and for the application of local content requirements or the provision of subsidies to locally produced services.

Throughout the history of the GATS, audiovisual services have probably been the most sensitive and most complex sector for negotiators. In fact, "negotiations in this sector have been delaying for up to a year the accession of a number of the newest WTO members."[6] At the end of the Uruguay Round, these proposals by the EC for a "cultural exception" in the GATS provoked a major crisis. When the United States refused, the European Union (EU), Canada, India, and many other countries simply invoked MFN exemptions on audiovisual services and did not schedule commitments in this sector. In fact, this sector is among those with the fewest commitments in GATS schedules. Cultural exceptions appear in regional (for example, NAFTA) and bilateral (for example, Canada-Chile) trade agreements.

The Latest Negotiation Proposals

Although no attempt was made to negotiate detailed sectoral trade rules for audiovisuals during the Uruguay Round, WTO members have tabled proposals regarding both the structure and content of the new negotiations, which started at the beginning of 2000 (commonly known as "Services 2000"). For example, Brazil[7] and Switzerland[8] tabled negotiating proposals on audiovisual services in 2001.

Brazil made three interrelated proposals, suggesting that members do the following:

- Make specific commitments in audiovisual services and, in doing so, give special attention to audiovisual services in which developing countries have great export potential (e.g., television services).

- Initiate a debate on subsidy schemes aimed at achieving national policy objectives of promotion and preservation of cultural identity and diversity.

- Initiate a debate in the framework of the GATS 2000 on trade defense and competition provisions to address unfair trade practices and restrictive business practices in the audiovisual services sector.

Brazil believes that the discussion on subsidies should take place in the ongoing negotiations on trade distortive subsidies (under Article XV of the GATS), and, given the disparities in members' capacities to subsidize, it should be ensured that such subsidies have the least trade distortive effect. It stresses that subsidy disciplines might not be sufficient in themselves to create real competition in certain areas, such as in motion picture production and distribution, in which the global market is characterized by an oligopolistic structure. Furthermore, in its view, the question of transfer pricing and the problem of placing audiovisual products on export markets at "dumping" price levels (because most of the production costs have been recouped on the home market of the producing company) should be seriously examined. Brazil argues that there seems to be a need to develop trade defense mechanisms (for example, specific antidumping disciplines) as well as competition disciplines in the audiovisual services sector.

Switzerland—referring to the fact that in the last services negotiations, many delegations treated this sector as an "all-or-nothing" issue (requesting full commitments or declining to make any)—seeks to start a debate that could lead to a more balanced approach. Members' individual concerns should be the starting point, and possible solutions should be discussed. The issues to be debated, in Switzerland's view, should include a cultural diversity safeguard, subsidies, public service, illicit content, competition issues, other regulatory issues and market access, and national treatment restrictions. On the basis of the debate, Switzerland would not preclude the possibility of setting up a specific multilateral trade policy framework for the audiovisual services sector.

The ongoing WTO round, referred to as the Doha Development Agenda negotiations, is expected to take up the thorny cultural exception issue again. The negotiations at the WTO would pit the conventional trade liberalization argument against the logic of cultural exception. The objective of the next GATS round and others that will follow is to add new services and sectors not previously listed under the commitments and to work toward removing trade-limiting regulations that were maintained by countries during previous rounds. The absence of commitments in broadcasting services in the Uruguay Round is considered to adversely affect one of the fastest growing distribution channels for U.S. audiovisual products.[9] However, because of the agreed-upon mechanism of making sector-specific offers and commitments, countries that have not scheduled any commitments in relation to audiovisual services are not obliged to accede to demands to do so. These countries reserve their right to impose new or more burdensome measures that may have a trade-limiting effect without penalty. Countries that have already included audiovisual services in schedules will be expected to undertake further liberalization of markets for these services. Countries that do not have cultural safeguards in place are likely to be especially vulnerable to pressures to schedule their audiovisual services sectors and commit to maintain open markets to foreign suppliers and products.

In addition to GATS negotiations, trade liberalization in audiovisual services is being exerted in other trade forums. The United States, for example, has a policy of pursuing trade liberalization in audiovisual services in bilateral treaties that it negotiates with other countries.

Maintaining a Restrictive Approach in the Audiovisual Services Sector?

The global dynamics of broadcasting coupled with new media technologies are likely to exert even stronger pressures for open international trade and the removal of domestic safeguard measures. As observed by the Organisation for Economic Co-operation and Development (OECD):

> Governments have traditionally used the licensing of broadcasting facilities to ensure the implementation of policy goals in respect to foreign and domestic content carriage. The restricted electromagnetic spectrum available for analogue transmission provided a technological rationale for the regulatory procedures that underpinned these policy goals. However, with the greater number of channels available for broadcasting which digital terrestrial over-the-air, satellite and cable technologies allow, the new environment makes a restrictive approach increasingly difficult to justify.[10]

Issues of safeguarding cultural autonomy and cultural identity are intensifying in an increasingly global environment. Audiovisual services industries, including television, film, disc, and video production, are organizing on transnational lines. In this environment, free trade proponents argue that there are important benefits from liberalizing audiovisual markets, especially for countries expanding new technologies and services. They argue that liberalized trade fosters investment as well as encourages adoption of new technologies and the development of more competitive domestic and foreign audiovisual services industries.[11] In particular, they highlight the domestic regulations that govern the movement of natural persons and investments, including foreign ownership and control regulations, as significantly limiting market entry.

The Issues Addressed in This Study

This monograph, the sixth in the American Enterprise Institute's series, Studies on Services Trade Negotiations, addresses many issues posed by the trends and developments within the area of trade in audiovisual services and among trade negotiators. The three authors—Patrick A. Messerlin,

Stephen E. Siwek, and Emmanuel Cocq—discuss different aspects of these issues.

Stephen E. Siwek examines the options for a changing course toward meaningful trade liberalization for entertainment products in the GATS. He analyzes in detail the specific market access and national treatment commitments made by the United States, Japan, and the EU in the audiovisual services under the GATS (see tables 2–4). He emphasizes in particular the role of positive commitments actually proposed by the trading partner, because the elimination of MFN exemption does not reflect actual commitments. He suggests the development of a wide-ranging negotiation strategy (led by the United States) in order to accelerate success in the audiovisual sector in the GATS. The following steps reflect Siwek's changing course toward trade liberalization for entertainment products in the GATS:

1. Develop a statistical dataset on content providers and ownership of media infrastructure facilities such as multiplex cinemas and broadcast stations.

2. Identify limits on market access and national treatment and prioritize new commitments from U.S. trading partners.

3. Initiate consultations under Article XV of the GATS in order to assess the level of foreign tax support and identify emerging subsidies.

4. Review MFN exemptions of "indefinite" duration with the basic exemption principles in the GATS Annex. (Although the GATS considers MFN exemptions to be temporary measures, the EU characterizes its cultural exemptions to MFN as "indefinite." However, indefinite subsidies in audiovisual products contradict the basic policies of the GATS.)

5. Develop a reference paper that focuses on the distribution of audiovisual products over the Internet. (Even though Siwek argues that the Internet is not likely to become like television in its role in mass media, he emphasizes that the Internet requires active participation in its use.)

Patrick A. Messerlin and Emmanuel Cocq focus on the profound economic changes (partly driven by technological changes) in importing countries, including the large EC film market. They argue that there are good reasons for optimism, and the initiative on trade and culture launched in the summer of 1999 by Canada (which pertains to the group of countries hesitant about liberalization of audiovisuals) is a first, though tenuous, sign of change.

The European Common Audiovisual Policies (CAPs) are as highly protective as the EC agricultural policy—and they increasingly show the same fatigue symptoms for essentially the same reasons. As a result, even though the CAPs are losing support among the public, large audiovisual firms, and regulatory agencies, which have some contact with markets, the EC and member state authorities still support them. In this regard, the authors provide a brief survey of the main instruments used by the CAPs: quotas, subsidies, and government-made monopolies. They claim that these instruments have balkanized EC audiovisual markets. The authors have drawn the following conclusions based on their study of the current status of the EC film markets:

- Broadcast quotas should be eliminated not only because of the usual static costs they impose on consumers, but also because they segment European markets and will become increasingly irrelevant with the coming technological changes.

- The policy frequently suggested currently in Europe (eliminate quotas, but keep all the public subsidies) is inappropriate. Existing policies (particularly in France) have shown that such an approach has left aside the "cultural" goal that was supposed to be the reason for subsidization. This has led to the customary "industrial subsidies," which have only succeeded in making European films and audiovisual works clones of the Hollywood productions.

- Eliminating industrial subsidies allows countries to concentrate on "cultural" subsidies, if they wish to do so. Defining cultural subsidies (that is, some commonly agreed-upon rules of competition) would be the key contribution of the reference paper to be drafted on audiovisuals in the context of WTO negotiations.

2

Changing Course:
Meaningful Trade Liberalization for
Entertainment Products in the GATS

Stephen E. Siwek

Even in Uruguay, the audiovisual sector remained a discomforting guest at the party. For services generally, the achievements of the Uruguay Round were unprecedented (as described in the introduction). But when the applause faded, the truth remained that in the GATS, the audiovisual services sector had again been left behind. The benefits of the sector-specific commitments made by only thirteen U.S. trading partners in audiovisual products do not offset the costs of perpetual discrimination and market limitation enshrined in the domestic policies of many others. Indeed, the undeniable fact of continued government support for discriminatory policies is neatly confirmed in the "indefinite" exemptions to MFN treatment in this sector that are listed in the relevant GATS schedules. More importantly, however, the MFN exemptions in audiovisual products listed by particular trading partners reflect only that part of the iceberg that is visible above the surface of the ocean.

A trading partner's decision to offer increased "market access" or "national treatment" in the GATS is reflected not in MFN exemptions but in the list of positive commitments actually proposed by that party. Unfortunately, in audiovisual products, many U.S. trading partners have either restricted or omitted entirely any positive commitment to liberalize trade in this industry. For example, the EU excludes any direct mention of audiovisual products in its list of specific commitments under the GATS. The EU's omission means that even if its MFN exemptions were to be removed, U.S. films and television programs would still face broadcast quotas within all EU markets. Similarly, the schedule of specific commitments listed by Japan for audiovisual products includes motion picture and videotape production and distribution services but omits any reference to television programming or transmission. For audiovisual products, the GATS today is hardly much of an improvement over the General Agreement on Tariffs and Trade (GATT) before the Uruguay Round.

Yet, recent trends in the distribution of audiovisual services around the world may provide some basis for optimism that the past will not be repeated. The recent emergence of the Internet as a potential medium for the distribution of video entertainment raises a host of additional issues for U.S. trade negotiators. In their policy statements relating to the Internet, both the United States and the EC have emphasized a "duty-free cyberspace" in order to encourage growth in global electronic commerce (E-commerce).[1] These parties have promised that the expansion of E-commerce will be market led and that new legal and regulatory barriers to the development of E-commerce will not be permitted. However, these statements consistently omit any pledge to oppose the expansion of discriminatory subsidies and quotas to the Internet. In its present form, the Internet has not yet achieved mass-market penetration in any consumer market anywhere. More to the point, it is extremely unlikely that the Internet will ever become a mass medium like television. For this reason, even if a trading nation sought to deny its people unfettered access to U.S. mass media, the enactment of subsidies and quotas specific to the Internet would do little to achieve this unfortunate goal. U.S. trading partners might nonetheless seek to impose culturally based discriminatory policies on the Internet because the Internet's potential in other respects may be perceived as too important to be left to the whims of the free market. By erecting the means to discriminate indefinitely over the Internet on cultural grounds, U.S. trading partners could seek to have the cake of "free cyberspace" and to eat it too.

Comprehensive trade reform in the audiovisual services sector is long overdue, and there are many issues that can be put on the table. Not all of these issues are equal in economic importance or equally likely to prevail. In addition, there are issues (such as cultural restrictions on Internet distribution of audiovisual products) for which the timing seems right even if the immediate impact is small. Accordingly, the United States should consider a wide-ranging strategy for changing the course of trade policy in the audiovisual services sector in the GATS.

First, the United States should develop comprehensive, country-by-country statistics and growth trends on the number of screens, the number of television broadcast channels, the number of cable and satellite

TV outlets, and the ownership status of media distribution entities around the world. Beyond the traditional content providers, these statistics should include data on ownership of media infrastructure facilities such as multiplex cinemas and broadcast stations. The United States should be armed with the right statistics to document how the world of entertainment has changed since the Uruguay Round.

Second, the United States should identify and prioritize the most burdensome limits on market access and national treatment that U.S. audiovisual producers now face, with the goal of securing new commitments in each such restriction in the upcoming GATS round.[2] For example, the United States might ultimately decide that Korea must make a specific commitment to reduce its screen quotas in this round. Alternatively, the United States could conclude that the EU must list a set of reduced broadcast quotas for films and programs of EU origin in a new specific commitment to improve market access under the GATS 2000. This process of identification and prioritization should begin immediately.

Third, consistent with its existing obligations, the United States should consider a request for consultations with major trading partners who maintain cultural subsidies of audiovisual products. These consultations, permitted under Article XV of the GATS, should be initiated in order to assess the level of foreign tax support that is earmarked for cultural media in major foreign markets and to identify emerging subsidies, particularly those that may offer discriminatory support for foreign media distribution over the Internet.

Fourth, the United States should consider challenging the continuation of all MFN exemptions for audiovisual products, including exemptions based on cultural considerations, in combination with its proposals for improved market access and national treatment. In particular, MFN exemptions of "indefinite" duration should be contested on the grounds that they are not consistent with the ten-year limits on MFN exemptions suggested as a basic principle in the GATS Annex on such exemptions.

Fifth, the United States should develop and release a reference paper that focuses on the distribution of audiovisual products over the Internet. The reference paper should analyze with some specificity whether and how the adoption of new policies specific to the Internet that discriminate against U.S. audiovisual products on cultural grounds might constitute a breach of the offending partner's MFN, market access, or national treatment obligations under the GATS.

Commitments and MFN Exemptions in the GATS

The GATS is the first ever set of multilateral, legally enforceable rules governing international trade in services. Like prior agreements on goods, such as the GATT, the GATS contains a main text that addresses basic principles and obligations, annexes dealing with rules for individual sectors, and specific commitments by individual countries to provide access to their markets. Unlike the GATT, the GATS has a fourth element: a set of exemption lists showing where countries are "temporarily" choosing not to apply the MFN principle of nondiscrimination. Importantly, the schedules and the exemption lists are integral parts of the GATS. At the time of the signature of the final act of the Uruguay Round on April 15, 1994, ninety-five schedules of specific commitments in services and sixty-one lists of derogations from the MFN principle had been submitted and agreed upon.[3] In addition to MFN, the basic principles of the GATS include national treatment, market access, transparency, and a commitment to progressive liberalization through further negotiation.

In the GATS, MFN and national treatment have distinct meanings. The principle of MFN means treating one's trading partners equally. By contrast, national treatment refers to equal treatment for foreigners and for one's own nationals. Importantly, a nation can choose to discriminate (at least temporarily) in its MFN obligations through the selective allowance of national treatment to the products and services of some trading partners but not to those of other trading partners. In the GATS, a commitment to national treatment applies only when a country has made a specific statement of that commitment, and exemptions to national treatment are allowed.[4] Departures from national treatment in the GATS are supposed to be clearly stated, be based on clearly established criteria, and service desirable policy objectives.[5] In addition to specific commitments to provide national treatment, trading partners can make specific commitments to improve market access. Article XVI of the GATS defines the following six types of mainly quantitative market access restrictions that shall not be maintained or adopted in respect to sectors in which market access commitments are undertaken unless specified otherwise in the schedule of specific commitments:[6]

- Limitations on the number of suppliers.
- Limitations on the total value of service transactions or assets.

- Limitations on the total number of service operations or on the total quantity of service output.

- Limitations on the total number of natural persons that may be employed.

- Measures that restrict or require specific types of legal entity or joint venture.

- Limitations on the participation of foreign capital.[7]

Within each schedule of specific commitments, trading partners list particular commitments (or limitations) to national treatment and market access in the following four discrete modes of supply:

- Cross-border supply.

- Consumption abroad.

- Commercial presence.

- Presence of natural persons.

Market Access and National Treatment Commitments in Audiovisual Services

Table 2 shows the GATS schedule of specific commitments made by the United States in audiovisual services. In the schedule, audiovisual services are divided into subsectors such as motion picture production and distribution services as well as radio and television services (for details, see introduction, page 3).

As shown in table 2, with the exception of radio and television services, the United States reports no limitations on access to its market for the audiovisual services of its trading partners. With respect to radio and television services, the United States does list market access limitations on the supply of audiovisual services requiring a commercial presence. These limitations include the requirement that only U.S. citizens may hold radio and television broadcast licenses as well as cross-ownership restrictions on a single company's ownership of newspapers and radio and TV broadcast stations serving the same local market. As regards U.S. limits on national treatment in audiovisual services, the U.S. schedule of commitments mentions only that grants from the National Endowment

TABLE 2
THE GATS SCHEDULE OF SPECIFIC COMMITMENTS MADE BY THE UNITED STATES

Audiovisual services sector or subsector	Limitations on national treatment[a]
Motion picture and videotape production and distribution	1) Grants from the National Endowment for the Arts are only available for individuals with U.S. citizenship or permanent resident alien status and nonprofit organizations. 2) None 3) Grants from the National Endowment for the Arts are only available for individuals with U.S. citizenship or permanent resident alien status and nonprofit organizations. 4) None
Motion picture projection services	1) None 2) None 3) None 4) None
Radio and television services	1) None 2) None 3) None 4) None
Radio and television transmission services	1) None 2) None 3) None 4) None
Sound recording services	1) None 2) None 3) None 4) None
Other audiovisual services	1) None 2) None 3) None 4) None

SOURCE: See United States International Trade Commission, "U.S. Schedule of Commitments under the General Agreement on Trade in Services" (USITC, May 1997), available at ftp://ftp.usitc.gov/pub/reports/studies/GATS97.pdf.

Limitations on market access[a]

1) None
2) None
3) None
4) Unbound except as indicated in HORIZONTAL COMMITMENTS

1) None
2) None
3) None
4) Unbound except as indicated in HORIZONTAL COMMITMENTS

1) None
2) None
3) None
4) Unbound except as indicated in HORIZONTAL COMMITMENTS

1) None
2) None
3) A single company or firm is prohibited from owning a combination of news-papers and radio and TV broadcast stations serving the same local market. Radio and television licenses may not be held by a foreign government; a corporation chartered under the law of a foreign country or that has a non-U.S. citizen as an officer or director or more than 20% of the capital stock of which is owned or voted by non-U.S. citizens; a corporation that is directly or indirectly controlled by a corporation of which more than 25% of capital stock is owned by non-U.S.citizens or a foreign government; or a corporation of which any officer or more than 25% of the directors are non-U.S. citizens.
4) Unbound, except as indicated in the HORIZONTAL SECTION. In addition, U.S. citizenship is required to obtain radio and television licenses.

1) None
2) None
3) None
4) Unbound except as indicated in HORIZONTAL COMMITMENTS

1) None
2) None
3) None
4) Unbound, except as indicated in the HORIZONTAL COMMITMENTS

a. Modes of supply: 1) cross-border supply, 2) consumption abroad, 3) commercial presence, and 4) presence of natural persons.

TABLE 3
THE GATS SCHEDULE OF SPECIFIC COMMITMENTS MADE BY JAPAN

Audiovisual services sector or subsector	Limitations on national treatment[a]	Limitations on market access[a]
Motion picture and videotape production and distribution services	1) None 2) None 3) None except as as indicated in HORIZONTAL COMMITMENTS 4) Unbound except as indicated in HORIZONTAL COMMITMENTS	1) None 2) None 3) None 4) Unbound except as indicated in HORIZONTAL COMMITMENTS
Motion picture projection services	1) Unbound 2) None 3) None except as indicated in HORIZONTAL COMMITMENTS 4) Unbound except as indicated in HORIZONTAL COMMITMENTS	1) Unbound 2) None 3) None 4) Unbound except as indicated in HORIZONTAL COMMITMENTS
Sound recording services	1) None 2) None 3) None except as indicated in HORIZONTAL COMMITMENTS 4) Unbound except as indicated in HORIZONTAL COMMITMENTS	1) None 2) None 3) None 4) Unbound except as indicated in HORIZONTAL COMMITMENTS

SOURCE: World Trade Organization, "Japan: Schedule of Specific Commitments," *General Agreement on Trade in Services*, GATS/SC/46, April 15, 1994, 40–41.
a. Modes of supply: 1) cross-border supply, 2) consumption abroad, 3) commercial presence, and 4) presence of natural persons.

for the Arts are available solely to U.S. citizens, permanent resident aliens, and nonprofit companies.

For purposes of comparison, table 3 presents the GATS schedule of specific commitments made by Japan in audiovisual services. Japan's schedule of commitments reports virtually no limits on market access or national treatment for three subsectors in audiovisual products.

These subsectors are motion picture and videotape production and distribution services, motion picture projection services, and sound recording services. The Japanese commitments do not extend, however, to radio and television services or to radio and TV transmission services. The failure on the part of the Japanese to make positive commitments in these important subsectors again shows that in the GATS it is often not what is listed but what is not listed that matters.[8]

The EU's schedule of specific commitments in audiovisual products is not included here because the EU made no specific commitments in audiovisual services (for details, see introduction, pages 5–6, as well as note 12 in this chapter).[9] For this reason, notwithstanding the efforts of U.S. negotiators in the GATS, the EU's market access restrictions in audiovisual products, including the Community's television broadcast quotas, remain in effect today. Note that for purposes of these agreements, separate nations within the EU are treated no differently than individual states within the United States. As a result, the EU's omission of specific commitments in audiovisual products means that even if the EU's MFN exemptions were to be eliminated (see below), U.S. films and television programs would still face broadcast quotas within all EU markets.

MFN Exemptions in Audiovisual Services

Although films and television programs are considered to be services in the GATS, they have a long and unfortunate history as "goods" within the context of the GATT. Article IV of the GATT specifically permitted the establishment and maintenance of screen quotas designed to guarantee that a minimum percentage of total screen time would be applied to the exhibition of films of national origin.[10] In many markets, U.S. distributors have also faced trade barriers and quotas that restricted the number of broadcast hours that could be devoted to American television programs.[11] In one form or another, these discriminatory policies have remained in force through the Uruguay Round and up to the present day.[12] Yet now, as in the past, major U.S. trading partners, including the EU and Canada, continue to defend subsidies and quotas in media products on the basis of subjective and nonquantifiable factors such as "cultural preservation" or the promotion of a "regional identity."[13]

Table 4 lists GATS exemptions to Article II (MFN) treatment for audiovisual services reported by the EC and its member states. As with specific

TABLE 4
THE EC AND ITS MEMBER STATES: MFN EXEMPTIONS IN AUDIOVISUAL SERVICES

Sector or subsector	Description of measure indicating its inconsistency with Article II
Audiovisual services: distribution of audiovisual works	Measures that may be imposed in order to respond to unfair pricing practices by certain third-country distributors of audiovisual works
Audiovisual services	Measures taken to prevent, correct, or counterbalance adverse, unfair, or unreasonable conditions or actions affecting EC audiovisual services, products, or service providers in response to corresponding or comparable actions taken by other members
Audiovisual services: production and distribution of audiovisual works through broadcasting or other forms of transmission to the public	Measures that define works of European origin in such a way as to extend national treatment to audiovisual works that meet certain linguistic and origin criteria regarding access to broadcasting or similar forms of transmission
Audiovisual services: production and distribution of cinematographic works and television programs	Measures based on government-to-government framework agreements (and plurilateral agreements) on coproduction of audiovisual works, which confer national treatment to audiovisual works covered by these agreements, in particular, in relation to distribution and access to funding
Audiovisual services: production and distribution of television programs and cinematographic works	Measures granting the benefit of any support programs (such as Action Plan for Advanced Television Services, MEDIA, or EURIMAGES) to audiovisual works, and suppliers of such works, meeting certain European origin criteria
Audiovisual services: distribution services	Waiver of the requirement in Spain to obtain licenses for the distribution of dubbed films of non-Community origin, granted to films of European origin that are especially recommended for children's audiences
Audiovisual services: television and radio broadcasting services	Foreign participation in companies in Italy exceeding 49% of the capital and voting rights, subject to a condition of reciprocity
Audiovisual services: production and distribution of cinematographic works and television programs in Nordic countries	Measures taken in Denmark that are adopted for the implementation of benefits in conformity with such support programs as the NORDIC FILM and TV FUND in order to enhance production and distribution of audiovisual works produced in Nordic countries

SOURCE: World Trade Organization, "European Communities and Their Member States: Final List of Article II (MFN) Exemptions," *General Agreement on Trade in Services*, GATS/EL/31, April 15, 1994, 1–3.
NOTE: Agreements already exist or are being negotiated with the following countries: Algeria; Angola;

Countries to which the measure applies	Intended duration	Conditions creating the need for the exemption
All members	Indefinite	Unfair pricing practices may cause serious disruption to the distribution of European works
All members	Indefinite (the need for exemption will lapse together with corresponding exemption from other members)	Need to protect the European Communities and their member states from adverse, unfair, or unreasonable unilateral actions from other members
Parties to the Council of Europe Convention on Transfrontier Television or other European countries with whom an agreement may be concluded	Indefinite (exemption needed for certain countries only until an economic integration agreement is concluded or completed)	The measures aim, within the sector, to promote cultural values both within EC member states and with other countries in Europe, as well as achieving linguistic policy objectives
All countries with whom cultural cooperation may be desirable (see note below)	Indefinite	The aim of these agreements is to promote cultural links between the countries concerned
European countries	Indefinite (exemption needed for certain countries only until an economic integration agreement is concluded or completed)	These programs aim to preserve and promote the regional identity of countries within Europe that have long-standing cultural links
Parties to the Council of Europe	Indefinite (exemption needed for certain countries until an economic integration agreement is concluded or completed)	The measure aims to promote European cultural values and linguistic policy objectives toward the youth
All countries	Indefinite	Need to ensure effective market access and equivalent treatment for Italian service suppliers
Finland, Norway, Sweden, and Iceland	Indefinite	Preservation and promotion of the regional identity of the countries concerned

Argentina; Australia; Brazil; Burkina Faso; Canada; Cape Verde; Chile; Côte d'Ivoire; Colombia; Cuba; Egypt; Guinea Bissau; India; Israel; Mali; Mexico; Morocco; Mozambique; New Zealand; São Tomé e Principe; Senegal; states in Central, Eastern, and Southeastern Europe; Switzerland; Tunisia; Turkey; and Venezuela.

commitments in the GATS, the MFN exemption lists divide audiovisual services into subsectors. Unlike lists of specific commitments, however, MFN exemptions require statements about the countries to which the exemptions apply, their intended duration, and the conditions creating the need for the exemption.

As shown in table 4, for many of its MFN exemptions, the EC intends that these measures exist indefinitely. The EU's MFN exemptions in audiovisual services include both responsive measures needed to respond to unfair pricing practices and other measures that discriminate (favorably) in the application of national treatment to the audiovisual products of other EU member states. The EU exemptions also include support programs for the supply of television programs and cinematographic works that meet European origin criteria. These support programs, such as Action Plan for Advanced Television Services, MEDIA, and EURIMAGES, aim to preserve and promote the "regional identity of countries within Europe which have long standing cultural links." The EU's intention to promote cultural "links" within Europe also extends to measures that define works of European origin for purposes of "access to broadcasting or similar forms of transmission."[14]

Table 5 provides GATS exemptions to MFN treatment for audiovisual services reported by Canada. These measures focus on differential treatment accorded to coproduction of films and television programs that intend to improve the availability of Canadian and Québécois audiovisual productions in Canada. As with the EC measures, the Canadian MFN exemptions are intended to be applied indefinitely.

Perhaps not surprisingly, even the United States is not free from MFN exemptions in audiovisual products. Table 6 provides excerpts from the MFN exemption list of the United States for telecommunications services.[15] The United States reports MFN exemptions in the one-way satellite transmission of direct-to-home (DTH) and direct broadcast satellite (DBS) television services and of digital audio services.[16]

This exemption in DBSs appears to permit the United States to retain the right to control which companies may broadcast from satellites into U.S. territory. Press reports suggest that the U.S. measure was aimed at Canada for refusing to relax certain restrictions on foreign ownership of Canadian assets.[17] Although it is possible to criticize the use of the GATS as a forum for purely bilateral trade negotiations, the broader point is that such focused restrictions are inherently less subjective than open-ended MFN exemptions that are rationalized on the basis of a perceived need to preserve a region's cultural identity. Bilateral disputes are capable, at least in principle, of a quid pro quo kind of resolution. The United States might, for example, remove these restrictions if Canada revised its rules on national ownership. Short of outright abandonment of a foreign market, is there a comparable set of focused actions that would convince the EU or the Canadians to eliminate cultural barriers in audiovisual products? If so, what might those actions be? A nation's inability, even in principle, to quantify the point at which it would consider the removal of cultural barriers is, at heart, what makes such barriers so pernicious.

Industry Growth and Non-U.S. Stakeholders in Audiovisual Products

Despite the difficulties inherent in any attempt to remove or eliminate cultural barriers in entertainment trade, all may not be doom and gloom for audiovisual services. In recent years, many markets in the world have experienced dramatic increases in the construction of new outlets for audiovisual products. This global expansion in media outlets has been driven by the widespread recognition on the part of both U.S. and non-U.S. investors that many audiovisual markets have had inadequate facilities to meet rising consumer demand. Although these construction trends comprise many types of audiovisual outlets, including multichannel cable television and satellite facilities, the recent boom can be seen most clearly in the worldwide growth of multiplex cinemas.

In June 1999, for example, the Commission Départementale d'Equipement Cinématographique (CDEC), a French regional cinema commission just outside Paris, approved three multiplex projects. One project in Torcy (18 screens, 3,750 seats) was proposed by a U.S. firm, AMC Entertainment; however, the other two projects, in Chelles (14 screens, 2,850 seats) and Claye-Souilly (14 screens, 3,850 seats), were proposed by the non-U.S. firms Village Roadshow of Australia and Pathé of France.[18] In the same period, CDECs in two other regions in France also approved multiplex proposals by Pathé and Village Roadshow. Although these projects may benefit U.S. audiovisual distributors, there is no doubt that they benefit non-U.S. interests as well.

Indeed, the ongoing growth in the construction of multiplex cinemas has not been limited to France. Peter Ivany, chief executive of Hoyts

TABLE 5
CANADA: MFN EXEMPTIONS IN AUDIOVISUAL SERVICES

Sector or subsector	Description of measure indicating its inconsistency with Article II
Film, video, and television programming coproduction	Differential treatment is accorded to works coproduced with persons of countries with which Canada may have coproduction agreements or arrangements and to natural persons engaged in such coproduction
Film, video, and television programming coproduction and distribution	Differential treatment is accorded to works coproduced with persons of countries with which Québec may have coproduction arrangements and to natural persons engaged in such coproductions as well as to natural and juridical persons engaged in film and video distribution pursuant to bilateral arrangements for the distribution of film, video, and television programming in its territory

SOURCE: World Trade Organization, "Canada: Final List of Article II (MFN) Exemptions," *General Agreement on Trade in Services*, GATS/EL/16, April 15, 1994, 1–5.

Corp. (another Australian company), recently estimated that if all cinema building goes forward as planned, "some 20,000 multiplex screens will be built worldwide in the next five to seven years at a cost of $10 billion to $15 billion."[19] Other non-U.S. multiplex leaders include Kinepolis of Belgium, Golden Harvest of Hong Kong, and Ster Kinekor of South Africa.[20]

The ongoing proliferation of movie screens around the world clearly provides more locations for both foreign and locally produced films to be viewed side by side. For this reason, in many foreign markets, local or regional films may now be able to achieve widespread exhibition even with free and unconstrained competition from U.S.-produced films. In addition, as noted above, many of the owners of these emerging multiplex cinemas are non-U.S. based. These non-U.S. firms will benefit from future increases in consumer demand for movies in foreign markets because demand for movies translates into demand for multiplex cinemas. And the maximum demand for movies in a given market can only be established

Countries to which the measure applies	Intended duration	Conditions creating the need for the exemption
All countries	Indeterminate	For reasons of cultural policy, including to improve the availability of Canadian audiovisual productions in Canada, to promote greater diversity among foreign audiovisual works on the Canadian market, and to promote the international exchange of audiovisual works
All countries	Indeterminate	For reasons of cultural policy, including to improve the availability of Québécois audiovisual productions in Québec, to promote greater diversity among foreign audiovisual works on the Québec market, to promote the international exchange of audiovisual works, and to ensure that Québec distributors have improved access to films originating from all parts of the world while allowing partners in film distribution arrangements to continue to distribute in Québec films for which they are recognized as the producers or the holders of the world distribution rights

in a free and unrestricted market. For this reason, emerging non-U.S. firms that invest in or benefit from free trade in audiovisual products may represent new stakeholders in the long-running debate over trade in audiovisual products. These non-U.S. firms clearly benefit from free trade in audiovisual products.

Limitations on Market Access and National Treatment

A trading partner's decision to offer increased "market access" or "national treatment" in the GATS is reflected not in MFN exemptions but in the list of positive commitments actually proposed by that party. For this reason, even if, for example, the EU were to remove its listed MFN exemptions in audiovisual products, U.S. films and television programs would still face broadcast quotas within all EU markets. As a result, U.S. negotiators should be particularly well versed in the market access

TABLE 6
THE UNITED STATES: EXCERPTS FROM THE MFN EXEMPTION LIST FOR
TELECOMMUNICATIONS SERVICES

(Private) sector or subsector	Description of measure indicating its inconsistency with Article II	Countries to which the measure applies	Intended duration	Conditions creating the need for the exemption
Telecommunication services: One-way satellite transmission of DTH and DBS television services and of digital audio services	Differential treatment of countries due to application of reciprocity measures or through international agreements guaranteeing market access or national treatment	All	Indefinite	Need to ensure substantially full market access and national treatment in certain markets

SOURCE: World Trade Organization, "The United States of America: List of Article II (MFN) Exemptions, Supplement 2," GATS/EL/90/Suppl.2, April 11, 1997, 2.

restrictions that actually apply in markets where positive commitments to provide market access in audiovisual products are conspicuous in their absence.

Markets that restrict U.S. audiovisual products exist in all regions of the world. In Korea, for example, cinemas are required to show Korean films 146 days out of the year on each screen, amounting to 40 percent of the year.[21] In Italy, published legislation imposes "seat and screen" quotas linked to the authorization required for new theaters under construction that exceed a seating capacity of 1,300.[22] In Indonesia, the Ministry of Information sets annual import quotas that restrict European and North American films.[23] In Australia, 50 percent of programming broadcast between 6:00 a.m. and midnight must be of Australian origin.[24] In Canada, all over-the-air television broadcasters must program at least 60 percent of their annual broadcast time with programming certified as Canadian content.[25] In China, there is evidence of an unwritten system of quotas for films, video, and television.[26] In addition to all of these examples, as discussed in the next section, the EU imposes European quotas on television broadcasting to all member states, which will be extended to Central and Eastern European countries as they apply for EU membership. Clearly, U.S. negotiators will face many markets where restrictions and barriers to audiovisual products can and should be identified. Ultimately, however, at the end of the negotiations, the challenge may be to narrow these targets to those where real progress can be achieved immediately.

Consultations on Audiovisual Subsidies

As noted earlier, the EU's audiovisual support programs such as MEDIA have been listed by the EC as "indefinite" exemptions to the MFN principle in the GATS. The idea that the EC should endeavor to support a European audiovisual industry dates back to the 1980s. In the latter part of that decade, Jacques Delors, president of the European Commission, committed the EU to the view that "culture [by which he meant European rather than French or German culture] is not merchandise like other commodities and it should not be treated as such."[27] On the basis of this view, in 1989, Delors proposed a program of assistance to European television and film production endowed with 250 million ECUs (250 million euros) over five years.[28] This endowment later became MEDIA. The MEDIA program adopted by the EC in December 1990 did not aim to subsidize film production directly. Instead, it sought to subsidize so-called "support" functions such as pilot projects, research, training, and exchange programs. Subsequently, in 1995 the EC proposed, and in December 1995 adopted, the MEDIA II program (1996–2000), which again focused on structural subsidies for development, distribution, and training in audiovisual works. The EC eventually allocated 310 million ECUs to MEDIA II.[29]

In a related development, on October 3, 1989, the EC adopted the Television Without Frontiers (TWF) directive, which held that the member states should ensure *"where practicable and by appropriate means* that broadcasters preserve a majority proportion of their transmission time for European works" (emphasis added).[30] Under the EC directive, the definition of "European" programs was complex. European content was determined on the basis of control of production, not on the basis of the source of material, directors, actors, or location. As a consequence, American studios could not generally expect their productions to qualify as European, except through coproduction. Even though certain member states have chosen to interpret liberally the "where practicable" caveat within the TWF directive, the directive remains at the heart of the EC's MFN exemptions, which define works of European origin for purposes of "access to broadcasting and similar forms of transmission."

In its GATS schedule, the EC clearly recognized that the Community's audiovisual subsidies and quotas were and are inconsistent with the MFN provisions of the Agreement. What seems to have been ignored, at least in the public debate, is that under the GATS, all MFN exemptions are to be reviewed after five years (in 2000) and should last no longer than ten years.[31] Whereas the GATS defines MFN exemptions as temporary measures, the EC characterized its cultural exemptions to MFN as "indefinite." Furthermore, the idea of unending MFN exemptions in audiovisual products was not limited to the Europeans. As already stated, both the Canadian and American MFN exemptions are also "indefinite" in duration.

The United States should consider a request for consultations regarding all indefinite subsidies in audiovisual products. Under Article XV, the United States should consider whether to seek to assess the level of foreign tax support that is earmarked for cultural media in major foreign markets under these subsidies and to identify emerging subsidies, particularly those that may offer discriminatory support for foreign media distribution over the Internet. The United States might attempt simply to end the most egregious of its indefinite subsidies (particularly in connection with Internet distribution of audiovisual products) and subsequently, if needed, include this as part of GATS negotiations in 2005. As a fallback position, the United States might simply raise these issues in order to negotiate more favorable terms on other issues such as market access and national treatment. The point remains, however, that indefinite subsidies in audiovisual products contradict the basic policies of the GATS.

In this context, also note that not only will the elimination of cultural subsidies benefit the foreign taxpayers who support these subsidies, but it will also benefit foreign producers and creators, who cannot now take full advantage of these subsidy programs. Not even cultural ministers can credibly deny that for the vast majority of products and services produced and distributed around the globe, market performance in a free market will generally exceed market performance in a subsidized market. World markets for films and television programs are not exceptions to this basic fact of life. Despite Delors' claims, films and television programs are commodities because they are subject to the laws of supply and demand. For this reason, in a subsidized media market, subsidy recipients likely will not include the correct mix of young and newly emergent creators who might otherwise revolutionize local television and film production in that market.[32] U.S. trade negotiators should not lose sight of these disenfranchised creators with whom they share a common goal. The forces of change and excellence in the film and television production industries of our trading partners do not always rise to the top in systems of quotas and subsidies.

Eliminating MFN Exemptions While Improving Market Access

The United States should develop a comprehensive set of proposals that combines the outright elimination of MFN exemptions, including cultural exemptions, for audiovisual products with the market access commitments discussed previously. Although market access and national treatment commitments may provide greater economic benefits, the United States should not abandon the argument that MFN exemptions to the GATS are inherently temporary in nature. Obviously, such a set of combined proposals would also mean that the United States itself could no longer use the GATS to force changes in Canadian foreign ownership rules (through restrictions on DBS transmissions) or Canadian tax laws (through differential treatment of tax deductions for broadcast advertising). Nevertheless, the end of MFN exemptions (in strict combination with new market access rights for audiovisual products) would likely lead to real economic benefits for U.S. film and television program creators and distributors.

For example, absent television subsidies and quotas, it is reasonable to conclude that the prices paid to U.S. television producers by European broadcasters would increase. No longer facing limits on the quantity of American programs they could air, European broadcasters would tend, all else being equal, to bid up the prices they would be willing to pay for U.S. programs. Additional benefits could result from changes in the mix of programs aired during prime time and from changes in the total programs purchased as European broadcast markets expanded. Beyond these considerations, absent subsidies and quotas, European consumers would be able to view the imported and domestic television programs that they really wanted to see. Free markets benefit consumers even in audiovisual products.

Cultural Discrimination and the Internet

In their policy statements relating to the Internet, both the United States and the EC have emphasized the benefits of a "duty-free cyberspace."[33] Mindful of the promise of E-commerce, these nations have agreed that the expansion of global E-commerce will be market led and driven by private initiative. The United States and the EC have stated, "The role of government is to provide a clear, consistent and predictable legal framework to promote a procompetitive environment in which electronic commerce can flourish and to ensure adequate protection of public interest objectives, such as privacy, intellectual property protection and public safety."[34] Thus, at the moment, the public interest objectives to be promoted over the Internet do not appear to include cultural preservation or the need to maintain a regional identity. Nevertheless, using even current digital technology, "virtually any image can be digitized, including books, newspapers, paintings, movies, TV programs, music, personal conversations, speeches, political cartoons, brainwaves, and three-dimensional objects."[35]

The United States and the EC have concluded that "unnecessary existing legal and regulatory barriers [affecting E-commerce] should be eliminated and that the emergence of new ones should be prevented."[36] Yet, paradoxically, in 1997, French Prime Minister Lionel Jospin announced a government initiative to accelerate his country's use of the World Wide Web. Specifically, Jospin described government subsidies to bring content from existing print media onto the Web and to support Internet-based tax payments, car ownership renewals, and employment searches.[37] More recently, when America Online (AOL) announced it would merge with Time Warner, it "stirred fear in France and elsewhere that the United States will secure an even greater cultural sway in the future by determining what Europeans will be able to see over the new medium."[38] In a world of "digital convergence," it seems only fair to ask whether the procompetitive, deregulatory commitments made by the United States and the EC will extend to audiovisual products and services that may be provided over or as part of the Internet. As of this writing, there is no clear evidence to suggest that they do, and that is precisely the point. If there is no clear evidence to suggest that our trading partners support an Internet that remains free of cultural restrictions, it is incumbent upon the United States to put that evidence in place. Now is the time to do this.

There are both technical and demand-related reasons to distinguish the Internet from traditional mass media. Despite its technical flexibility, "the Internet is optimized for e-mail and data files. . . . "[39] Using the Internet also requires both a computer and a personal desire to be entertained through the active participation in a medium. Television watching requires neither. For these reasons, in its present form, it is extremely unlikely that the Internet will ever become a mass medium like television.[40] If the Internet is not destined to become a mass medium, then one need not worry that the Internet will ever "threaten" the culture of a trading partner or region. Indeed, even if a trading nation sought to deny its people unfettered access to U.S. mass media, the enactment of subsidies and quotas specific to the Internet would do little to achieve this unfortunate goal.

How then could our trading partners rationalize cultural restrictions on the Internet? Suppose that, over time, the Internet evolves to become one of many media over which audiovisual products may be distributed to a few selected users. These few users would need high-capacity telecommunications links and specialized data storage devices. Except for these users, the Internet could be characterized (incorrectly as it turns out) as "a similar form of transmission" to broadcasting. In this scenario, policymakers who may have other reasons to regulate the Internet could then ignore the interactive, non–mass market character of the Internet. Indeed, one can readily imagine an information minister who decides that the potential of the Internet for E-commerce is too important to be left to the whims of the free market. What better way to assert government control over this emerging medium than to impose access restrictions based on the subjective need to promote cultural or regional identity. By enacting access restrictions or other means of cultural discrimination for the Internet, our trading partners could seek to have the cake of "free cyberspace" and to eat it too.

In describing the Global Electronic Commerce initiative, U.S. officials observed that the principle of tariff-free cyberspace "needs to be established quickly, before nations impose tariffs and vested interests mobilize to protect those tariffs."[41] The same argument applies here. The Internet should be kept free of the myriad quotas, access restrictions, and subsidies that have plagued the audiovisual sector throughout the twentieth century. If the United States fails to act, the result could easily be the imposition of new means of discrimination in the emerging digital technologies that will flourish in the century to come.

3

Preparing Negotiations in Services: EC Audiovisuals in the Doha Round

Patrick A. Messerlin and Emmanuel Cocq

Introduction

Under the 1994 Uruguay Round Agreement, only nineteen WTO members have made commitments in audiovisual services in their GATS schedule (see table 7).

As illustrated in table 7, these commitments are generally of limited scope and magnitude.[1] Among the large audiovisual producers, only the United States has taken substantial commitments at the various stages of audiovisual production, distribution, and transmission. Although more limited, the commitments by India (the world's largest film producer), Hong Kong, and Japan show the acceptance by countries with large production and influential cultures to consider the issue of liberalization in audiovisual services with an open mind. The rest of the WTO members, led by the EC, have severely limited the access to their markets because they are insecure about the ability of their audiovisual industry to compete, they want to minimize the exposure of their people to foreign influence (France), or they want to use audiovisual services as an instrument for building their national identity (Australia and Canada).

If negotiations for services followed the same pattern as those for goods, WTO negotiators would try to solve such conflicting approaches among WTO members by striking intersectoral trade-offs. For instance, the EC water utilities or Canadian lumber firms would lobby their own authorities for removing EC or Canadian barriers in audiovisuals (as concessions to be granted for getting better access to U.S. water or lumber markets), whereas the U.S. audiovisual services sector would lobby the U.S. government for the opening of maritime transportation (as concessions to be traded for getting better access to EC or Canadian audiovisual markets). However, these intersectoral trade-offs may be a component of WTO negotiations in services, but probably not to the same extent as in goods. As a result, the inclusion of

TABLE 7
SUMMARY OF SPECIFIC COMMITMENTS IN AUDIOVISUAL SERVICES UNDER THE URUGUAY ROUND

Countries	Film and video production and distribution CPC: 96112, 3	Film projection services CPC: 96121, 2	Radio and TV services CPC: 96131, 2, 3	Radio and TV transmission services CPC: 75241, 2	Sound recording CPC: n.a.	Other CPC: 96114	Total
Large producers (by decreasing number of films produced)							
India	X						1
United States	X	X	X	X	X	X	6
Hong Kong	X				X	X	3
Japan	X	X			X		3
Smaller producers							
Central African Republic	X	X	X	X	X	X	6
Dominican Republic				X		X	2
El Salvador				X		X	2
Gambia	X	X	X	X			4
Israel	X						1
Kenya	X	X					2
Korea	X				X		2
Lesotho	X	X	X	X			4
Malaysia	X			X			2
Mexico	X	X					2
New Zealand	X	X	X	X		X	5
Nicaragua	X	X					2
Panama	X	X	X		X		4
Singapore	X				X		2
Thailand	X		X				2
Total	17	10	7	8	7	6	55

SOURCE: World Trade Organization, *Audiovisual Services*, Table 9 S/C/W/40 (Geneva: WTO, 1998).
NOTE: CPC: Central Product Classification.

audiovisuals as one of the services to be liberalized during the Doha Round has so far been received by skepticism in WTO circles.

However, there are good reasons for optimism, as stressed in the postscript (see page 54), and recent developments in audiovisuals have confirmed this view. Optimism flows from ongoing profound economic changes, partly driven by technological changes. These changes are largely procompetitive and require larger markets, including in the EC, which is the focus here. Meanwhile, the highly protective European Common Audiovisual Policies (CAPs) increasingly show the same fatigue as EC agricultural policy—broadly for the same reasons—and face a significant erosion of public support. All these converging forces make the option of market opening in the audiovisual services sector increasingly attractive.

Audiovisuals in the Doha Round: *Mission Impossible?*

Reciprocity—the traditional negotiating tool in trade rounds—will be of limited use for services, including audiovisuals. First, it cannot be easily measured. Negotiators have no tools to assess whether liberalizing audiovisual services will be worth roughly the same value as, for example, liberalizing maritime transport or water utilities. (In the case of goods, evaluating the concessions received and granted relies on the tariff reductions received and granted, weighted by the trade values involved.)

Second, reciprocity has a much vaguer meaning in services than in goods. Removing a tariff is often enough to change substantially pricing behavior, entry, and exit in product markets. This is not necessarily the case for services, for which liberalization requires deep domestic regulatory reforms.

Difficulties for negotiators do not start with considerations about culture. They emerge in the very first steps of evaluating the concessions offered by the various trading partners, and they are common to all services. For instance, reliable data on imports require "rules of origin," which allow a clear distinction between imported and domestic products and between products imported from different countries. Such a concept is not easily applicable to all services, including audiovisual services. For instance, defining a "domestic" film is not a simple matter, and differences in definitions can lead to huge differences when assessing the scope and evolution of the audiovisual services sector. The French Centre National de la Cinématographie (CNC) has three alternative rules of origin for defining French films: "French-initiative films," which include "100 percent French films" and "French majority co-productions"; "Foreign majority co-productions"; and "approved films." From 1997 to 2001, an average of 108 films were produced under the narrower definition (100 percent French films) and an average of 150 films were produced under the wider definition (approved films). Rules of origin are so complex that they can easily lead to arbitrary decisions, recently illustrated by *The*

Fifth Element, which was defined as an integrally French movie because it had been largely financed by a French studio. However, it was shot in London and in English, and employed many non-French actors—all infringements to normal conditions for obtaining status as an integrally French movie (in fact, there is an ongoing legal suit against this decision to grant French origin).

Moreover, negotiations in audiovisual services present specific obstacles, the most prominent being the strong link perceived between audiovisual services and "national culture" by many GATS members. However, the paradox is that the existing regulatory policies that allegedly support national culture tend to harm it profoundly. For instance, the French audiovisual policy has strongly induced French filmmakers to mimic U.S. filmmakers, leading to an accelerated "Americanization" of French culture. The fact that this paradox is increasingly perceived in Europe removes an obstacle to liberalization.

In such a delicate context, negotiators will be strongly pressured by audiovisual firms, which are very diverse. Whereas some of these companies operate almost exclusively in the audiovisual services sector of their countries (such as publicly owned audiovisual firms), others have internal potential sectoral trade-offs. For example, Bertelsmann is a large German-based press firm that owns a large audiovisual services sector in several OECD countries. The same could still be said for Vivendi, a French firm, although there are doubts about the long-term sustainability of its strategy.

Technological and Economic Changes: *The Quantum Project*[2]

Technology is profoundly changing audiovisual markets, inducing the most dynamic EC firms to make drastic revisions to their strategies—to the point of being much more open to unilateral regulatory reforms. Following is a quick survey of these changes.

As is well known, technical progress in telecoms is generating profound changes in audiovisuals, and this convergence process is far from over. The digital revolution in telecoms will reduce a government's ability to protect domestic audiovisual markets. For instance, the EC quota on non-European movies on TV (40 percent of all broadcast movies) will become obsolete when EC TV viewers are able to download movies at a reasonable cost from a satellite dish through the Internet or from terrestrial digital TV, allowing free cross-border diffusion between EC member states. New technology will make it possible for each EC broadcaster to fulfill the current obligation of permanently supplying 40 percent of domestic films (if only by buying audiovisual flops produced in large quantities by the massive subsidies available in the CAPs), whereas European TV viewers will download only foreign films supplied by this company.

Technological change has generated economic changes. It has forced EC firms willing to survive as world players to reassess the contours of the markets relevant to them and to realize that they are too small in global markets. Table 8 shows that in 1997 the average size (in terms of audiovisual turnover) of the twenty-three largest EC firms was half the average size of the fifteen largest U.S. firms.

Size matters in the audiovisual services sector because it is one of the riskiest parts of a modern economy. A large firm can implement several strategies of risk management more easily than a smaller firm. These strategies can include launching several films (hoping that the profitable ones will compensate for the losses of the others); releasing films on video, DVD, and other formats; and marketing brands by using the same concept in, for example, a film, a TV series, a book, a magazine, clothes, and toys (to increase revenues).

Table 8 suggests that EC firms are significantly more specialized in audiovisual services and hence more fragile during the inevitable downturns. It also suggests that EC firms tend to be smaller and less diversified in the EC member states enforcing the most restrictive CAPs. This correlation mirrors a true causality. Most EC protectionist measures in audiovisual services have consisted of taxing consumers or creating monopolies—two sure recipes for inhibiting market growth. The more strictly the CAPs have been enforced, the more the markets have been severely segmented and restrained, or balkanized, and the smaller the EC firms have tended to be. Moreover, the fact that size counts much less for "cultural" films and TV shows (such works tend to require less funds, making their risks more easily bearable) implies that most EC firms are too small for entertainment and too big for culture.

However, because EC audiovisual firms tend to be monopolies in member state markets, they have become the target of the European competition authorities for "abuse of dominant power." Mergers in EC audiovisual services represent 2 percent of the total number of EC mergers, but the ban of mergers in audiovisual services by EC competition authorities amounts to half of all the merger bans decided. Similar observations can be made at the member state level. For instance, the largest French firm (Canal Plus) was fined for excessive market power in film catalogue (the

TABLE 8
COMPARISONS OF LEADING U.S. AND EC AUDIOVISUAL FIRMS, 1996–1997

Country	Audiovisual turnover Millions USD 1996	Total turnover Millions USD 1997	Audiovisual turnover Millions USD 1997	Growth rate in audio. turnover (%) 1997/1996	Audiovisual in total turnover (%) 1997	Net results Millions USD 1997	Net results in percent of turnover 1997	Audiovisual turnover per inhabitant 1997
The 23 European firms among the 50 leading world firms								
Austria (1 firm)	942	818	818	–13.2	100.0	26.5	3.2	101.0
Britain (7 firms)	14,927	27,081	17,170	15.0	63.4	1,504.3	8.8	293.5
France (4 firms)	6,085	5,896	5,602	–7.9	95.0	353.1	6.3	96.4
Germany (7 firms)[a]	19,177	27,872	18,904	–1.4	67.8	1,169.8	6.2	230.8
Italy (2 firms)	5,049	4,855	4,855	–3.8	100.0	476.8	9.8	84.9
Luxembourg (1 firm)	2,683	3,189	2,910	8.5	91.3	–80.6	–2.8	ns[b]
Netherlands[c] (1 firm)	5,628	5,686	5,686	1.0	100.0	403.3	7.1	277.4
All	54,491	75,397	55,945	2.7	74.2	3,853.2	6.9	196.6
All in 1996 (23 firms)	53,356	72,890	54,269	1.7	74.5	3,234.9	6.0	190.7
The 15 U.S. firms among the 50 leading world firms								
All	64,557	230,583	73,491	13.8	31.9	14,009.4	19.1	279.4
All in 1996 (13 firms)	49,055	95,365	63,416	29.3	66.5	4,653.2	7.3	241.1

SOURCE: European Audiovisual Observatory, *Statistical Yearbook* 1999 (Strasbourg, France), 69.
a. Net results are not available for Kirch, RTL, and SAT1.
b. Not significant.
c. Including Belgian Flemish-speaking population.

list of films on which it can levy fees for intellectual property rights) because (in accordance with the existing audiovisual regulations) the relevant market has been defined by the French competition authorities as the French-speaking film market, that is, 40 percent of the French market—a small proportion of an already relatively small market by world standards. In summary, EC firms have been kept smaller than they could have been because CAPs balkanize national markets.

Despite their small size and their inability to grow because of market balkanization, EC audiovisual firms have been a good buy for other firms because of their monopoly rents. Most of them have thus become integrated in companies involved in other activities, for instance, press and publishing (Bertelsmann, Canal Plus-Havas, Fininvest, and Kirch), advertising (Canal Plus-Havas and Fininvest), insurance (Fininvest), telecoms (Bertelsmann), and utilities (Canal Plus-Vivendi).

The recent integration of EC audiovisual firms in larger firms with a wider set of production activities is dramatically changing the balance of coalitions that could support the Doha Round. Being a profound departure from the traditional European scheme of public monopolies highly specialized in audiovisual services, it is likely to influence the debate about culture in two ways. First, it enlarges the vision about "cultural goods," fudging the economically wrong (but politically powerful) debate about trade balances. For instance, today, the negative EC trade balance in films is a powerful argument for protection (even though economically it does not make sense). A wider view about all cultural goods produced by firms like Bertelsmann or Vivendi will balance the negative EC trade balance in films by the positive EC trade balance in books or magazines, helping to diffuse the pressures on cultural protection. Second, EC firms looking for access to foreign markets for their nonaudiovisual activities will be less hostile to the opening of EC audiovisual markets. Most of the large European groups owning audiovisual firms are in such a situation.

Audiovisual Services in the EC: *Titanic*

This section provides a brief survey of the main instruments—quotas and subsidies—used by the CAPs and an economic analysis of their effects. Although it draws many examples from France, it reflects the overall situation in the EC for two reasons. First, almost all other EC member states (including "free trade–minded" countries, such as Britain) have adopted or maintained audiovisual measures relatively similar to the French ones.[3] Second, the complex process of generating European, "supra-national" regulations is further eroding differences among member states. For instance, in November 1998, the French TV regulator (Conseil Supérieur de l'Audiovisuel [CSA]) decided not to impose

French legal constraints on TV channels from other EC member states but to submit them to the EC regime.

Quotas: *A bout de souffle.* The Television Without Frontiers (TWF) European Directive (adopted in 1989 and amended on June 30, 1997 by the European Directive 97/36/EC) imposes "broadcast" quotas based on film nationality. It stipulates "that broadcasters reserve for European works . . . a majority proportion of their transmission time, excluding the time appointed to news, sports events, games, advertising, teletext services and teleshopping." The Directive, however, specifies that "member-states shall ensure this principle where practicable and by appropriate means."[4] These quotas are rigidly enforced in certain member states (for example, France) and more subtly implemented in the other member states—but not necessarily with less consequences, as best illustrated by the almost identical shares of U.S. fiction TV shows in Britain and France.[5]

Broadcast quotas are combined with other quantitative restrictions in certain member states. In France, for instance, "global" quotas limit the total number of films that can be broadcast per year, and time-specific quotas prohibit the broadcasting of films on most TV channels on certain days and hours. These quotas are set to protect cinemas from competition by TV channels.[6] Quotas on investments require every TV channel to invest a share of its resources in film production by "prepurchasing" or "coproducing" films, that is, 3 percent of the net turnover for French TV channels, 20 percent in the Canal Plus case (out of which 9 percent are French films). Furthermore, there are additional rules imposing constraints on how quickly a movie done for theaters can be programmed on TV channels and sold as videos. These rules (which have been loosened in recent years) have the same effect as quotas; that is, they artificially segment markets.

From an economic perspective, the key question is whether or not these quotas are binding. The answer is no for the French quotas on the total number of films that can be broadcast annually. These quotas have been substantially increased over time, and they are close to the number of broadcast films in EC member states not enforcing such a restriction. However, the answer is yes for EC-based broadcast quotas on U.S. films. For example, these quotas are strongly binding in France, where U.S. films have a market share greater than 40 percent (ranging from 53 to 63 percent during the 1990s) in cinemas where French viewers can make free choices.[7] Similarly, investment quotas that contribute to increased production of French films are binding.

TABLE 9
EUROPEAN PUBLIC SUPPORT FOR FILM AND AUDIOVISUAL WORKS, 2000

	Total million euros	Production[a] %	Distribution %	Exploitation %
Austria	16.4	90	10	
Belgium	18.4	92.4	7.6	
Britain	57.5	96.5	1	2.5
Denmark	23.3	91	8.2	0.8
Finland	12.4	90	4.4	5.6
France	368.1	82.1	5.4	12.5
Germany	149.6	90	8.4	1.6
Greece	3.8	100	0	0
Ireland	8	99	1	0
Italy	94.5	89.9	10.1	0
Netherlands	34	99.4	0.6	0
Portugal	17.2	92.2	0	7.3
Spain	80	98.6	1.1	0.3
Sweden	36.7	78	22	[b]
EC-15	921.3	88.3	6.2	5.5

SOURCE: European Audiovisual Observatory, *Statistical Yearbook* 2002, vol. 3 (Strasbourg, France), 102.
a. Includes scriptwriting and development schemes and project development.
b. Support for exhibition is included in distribution.

However, these instruments of protection have not had the expected positive impact on French films. For instance, not enough French films are produced to meet the quota of French films to be broadcast during TV prime time. From 1994 to 2001, there have been, on average, only eleven French films per year having enough success in cinemas (more than one million viewers) to be candidates for broadcast during prime time—compared with an average of twenty-four U.S. films. As a result, TV channels increasingly show reruns of old French films (the rerun rate has increased from less than 60 percent in the 1980s to 70 percent in the 1990s) to meet the annual 40 percent quota of French films and fiction TV works—relegating recent French films to late or early hours of the day.

Subsidies: *Men in Black.* Table 9 shows that all EC member states implement massive subsidy schemes. In 2000, with supports amounting to 368 million euros for films and audiovisual works (films made for TV channels in EC jargon), France outdistanced other European countries. (In what follows, euros will be used for ECUs as well as for euros.) Since 1997, the gap has somewhat narrowed. In 2000, the amount of the

TABLE 10
SUBSIDIZATION RATES OF THE FRENCH FILM INDUSTRY, 1995–2000

M€, annual average during the period	Estimate 1	Estimate 2
Public aid to cinema	187.7	318.9
Movie theater income of French films	259.6	259.6
TV income of French films	326.6	195.4
Video income of French films	69.3	69.3
Export income of French films	82	82
Average subsidies rate of French films	25.5%	52.6%

SOURCE: Centre National de la Cinématographie, *Annual Reports*, 1995–2000 (Paris); authors' calculations.

French subsidies represented 39.9 percent of total European funds, compared with 45.6 percent in 1997. Nevertheless, French public support still exceeds by far the support granted by Germany, Britain, Italy, and Spain, all countries known for their interventionist policies on this matter. Note that table 9 underestimates the differences between France and the other EC member states because the figures provided on French public support do not fully take into account the implicit support imposed by the investment quota regime (which is much more important in France than in any other European country).

Table 10 addresses this implicit subsidy issue for French films (excluding audiovisual works) for the period between 1995 and 2000.[8] It gives two estimates of the subsidization rate, which differ with their treatment of the income that film producers derive from TV purchases. Estimate 1 includes in the film industry income the full expenses on purchased and prepurchased films made by TV channels. However, part of these TV purchases are imposed by the regulatory framework, namely broadcasting and investment quotas. This component should thus be considered as implicit subsidies granted by TV channels to French film producers. Because it ignores this more appropriate interpretation, estimate 1 undervalues somewhat the subsidization rate to French films. Estimate 2 aims to correct this bias by using Cocq's estimate,[9] according to which 41 percent of broadcasters' investments are imposed by the existing regulations. Consequently, 131.2 million euros should be deducted from the income from TV channels and reported as public support.

Table 10 suggests that during the late 1990s, the subsidization rate of the French cinema exceeded 50 percent, according to the unbiased estimate 2. However, this rate is likely to be substantially lower than the true rate because it is based on film revenues (and not on the added value, as it should be) and it does not take into account a variety of funds, in particular SOFICA's tax-based incentive scheme for private investment in film production, and—much more importantly—Canal Plus monopoly rent. With an average spending of 130 million euros per year in the late 1990s, Canal Plus alone contributed to two-thirds of all funds flowing from investment quotas.[10] This huge investment requirement has been explicitly conceived as a counterpart of the monopoly granted to Canal Plus for broadcasting films in pay TV. In the 1990s, the monopoly rents that Canal Plus could extract from its French TV viewers was estimated to be 300 million euros per year, meaning that almost half of Canal Plus monopoly rents is an indirect way of taxing French TV viewers in order to subsidize French film producers.[11] If one adds all these subsidies, the rate of subsidization of French films is close to 100 percent.

This regime deserves a last, but crucial, observation. Skyrocketing subsidies have profoundly shaped film production away from culture. The standardization of "automatic" production subsidies calculated on admissions in cinemas, introduced by the "Plan Lang" (from former Culture Minister Jack Lang) in 1989, has fueled the production of French "entertainment" films mimicking high-cost Hollywood movies. Combined with broadcast quotas, such subsidies have protected French-made Hollywood clones from their Hollywood competitors, leading to an accelerated "Americanization" of the French film output and hurting the production of cultural films—all the more because the very limited subsidies for such movies are granted by quasi-corporatist committees favoring the fashion of the time more than creativity.

Winners and Losers: *Four Funerals and a Wedding*

European CAPs are so complex that operators in audiovisual markets want to stick to the status quo simply because they cannot assess whether they will lose or gain in the case of reforms. Fear of being among the net losers of liberalization nurtures everybody's hostility to reforms, whereas the complexity of the protection is likely to have generated so many inefficiencies that everybody is already a net loser. For instance, the French version of the EC system of quotas, subsidies, and monopoly rents (created, then taxed and transferred) involves at least six different participants: cinema owners, film producers (foreign, French successful, and French unsuccessful), broadcasters, and French consumers.

Most of these operators do not know whether the existing regime makes them net winners or losers. Cinema owners benefit from the quota on the total number of films to be broadcast and from the subsidies (both increase demand for cinema seats), whereas they bear the cost of the 11 percent seat tax, which reduces this demand. U.S. filmmakers face the seat tax and the 40 percent broadcast quota on U.S. films (both reduce the demand of their films), but they recoup a portion of the seat tax to the extent that they are the main beneficiaries of the relatively comfortable French cinemas. EC filmmakers face the same situation as U.S. film producers, with two differences: They have access to French subsidies, but they are unlikely to benefit from possible rents associated with the quota on EC films (their demand by French TV viewers is too limited). Successful French film producers share many features with EC filmmakers, and they get even more subsidies, leaving them with the impression of being major beneficiaries (but perhaps wrongly, because their situation in the absence of CAPs could be even better). Broadcasters are "taxed" by investment quotas (and by taxes or fees on their advertising resources), but they may benefit from these quotas to the extent that they provide some flexibility in programming. Canal Plus is an extreme case, with huge monopoly rents constrained by investment quotas (with the rise of its competitor TPS increasingly deteriorating Canal Plus's net situation to the point that it could become a net loser in the future).

There is only one group of sure winners and one group of sure losers. Unsuccessful French filmmakers are unambiguously net winners: They are not hurt by the seat tax (nobody wants to see their movies), and they are fully subsidized. The larger their budgets are, the more they are winners. Ironically, big-budget unsuccessful French-made clones of Hollywood films get the best of the EC-French system. By contrast, the viewers of French films and the French taxpayers are unambiguously net losers. They are taxed directly (when funding subsidies) or indirectly (when going to movie cinemas or when subscribing to Canal Plus), and French viewers who want to see U.S. films are hurt by restrictions on these films, whereas French viewers interested in cultural films are hurt by minimal public support for this category of films.

A System Slowly Losing Its Support: *Titanic, Part II*

In the late 1990s, the perception of the CAPs enforced in some member states since the early 1980s, and generalized with the 1989 TWF European Directive, dramatically changed. A profound sense of dissatisfaction has emerged in all the member states, particularly in those implementing strict CAPs, such as France. What follows documents this evolution, underlining the fact that the much-publicized statement made in December 2001 by Jean-Marie Messier, then head of Vivendi-Universal, that "the Franco-French cultural exception is over," is the end result of a long process.

The unfairness of certain rules (and the ease with which they can be manipulated by committees) has been the first source of increasing criticism, as illustrated by the disputes on rules of origin discussed previously. A few years ago, movies unduly classified as French films were denounced in carefully balanced terms by Cour des Comptes but with no public echo.[12] In 1997, the above-mentioned highly controversial case of *The Fifth Element* was widely covered by the film specialized press (which is closely following the ongoing legal battle).

In 1998, the procedure for granting French origin to movies was reformed, with the language criterion losing some of its influence. But the changes have only generated new problems, as illustrated by a few recent cases. In 2000, a Japanese-made cartoon was presented as a French movie, fueling fierce criticisms in *Le Monde*.[13] More recently, the film *Un long dimanche de fiançailles*, directed by Jean-Pierre Jeunet (the director of the very successful *Le fabuleux destin d'Amélie Poulain*), almost did not receive French origin—despite the fact that it was shot in French and in France, with French actors—because the producer of the film (Production 2003) was a 40 percent subsidiary of the U.S. firm Warner.[14] Opponents to granting French origin to the movie in question argued that providing French subsidies to subsidiaries of U.S. filmmakers signified the end of the French cultural exception. Meanwhile, the movie *Alexander the Great* by Oliver Stone (a U.S. director with a French passport) was shot in English, with U.S. and British actors, but received French origin without problem, even though it was funded by the French firm Pathé only up to 20 percent.

Dissatisfaction has then grown concerning the production performance of the CAPs. During the early years of the system (the 1980s), the high number of films produced was perceived as a sign of success of the

French audiovisual policy—it was an essential argument for "selling" the French regime to the other EC member states. Of course, the fact that French film production remained high—while film production was declining (sometimes dramatically) in other EC member states—simply mirrored the fact that more French public money was made available to filmmakers and spent by them (once again, not necessarily for a cultural purpose). As time went on and other EC member states implemented their own version of the CAPs, their film industries began to produce roughly the same number of films as France (between 80 and 130 films per year for the largest member states), leading to the realization in Europe that this indicator was largely meaningless.[15]

The disenchantment was then followed by a spreading recognition of the uselessness of broadcast quotas in Europe, as underlined by the EC Commission: "There [is] a pretty general consensus that broadcast quotas no longer suited the new environment."[16] This perception has penetrated even the member states that have been historically the most attached to this instrument. A series of interviews about audiovisual regulations before the Seattle WTO Ministerial revealed a definite change of tone in France.[17] Patrick Le Lay, head of the largest (private) TV channel, TF1, was very clear about the fact that quotas have been made "obsolete" by digitalization and the Internet, whereas Marc Tessier, head of the public channel France Télévision, and Pierre Lescure, head of Canal Plus, were in favor of "more flexibility" of the existing regime, leaving only Rémy Sautter, head of CLT-UFA, in favor of quotas (but not of subsidies).

Declining public support for the quota regime in recent years mirrors the increasing share of foreign films in cinema admissions. Until the late 1990s, the diverging evolutions of the shares of U.S. and domestic films in France and other European countries (see table 11) were perceived as the sign of success of the French film policy. In fact, however, as said above, the high market share of domestic films in France was the mere consequence of the massive French subsidies, relative to the support granted by other countries.

However, this difference has been vanishing during recent years, and market shares of films by nationality tend to converge in all EC member states (see table 12). The same can be said for the market shares for domestic films (the dubious classification of The Fifth Element as a French film increases the 1997 French film market share in France by 5 percentage points), and the recognition of a "commercial rout" in 1999 has been widely acknowledged in the French press.[18]

TABLE 11
EC Audiovisual Markets: Cinemas, TV Channels, and Videos, 1996–1997

	Theaters[a]		TV channels[b]		Videos	
	U.S. films	EC films	U.S. films	U.S. fiction works	VCR penetration rate[c]	Blank cassettes[d]
	1994–97	1997	1996	1996	1997	1997
Austria	—	0.0	64.6	26.6	75.3	4.7
Belgium	71.9	0.1	34.1	31.1	68.4	4.1
Britain	80.5	4.8[e]	75.3	19.8	83.0	3.1
Denmark	70.2	0.2	65.6	27.4	79.0	5.0
Finland	72.7	0.1	67.0	14.8	72.2	4.4
France	55.7	10.2	36.2	18.9	77.5	6.3
Germany	78.6	3.7	65.2	35.5	77.3	3.4
Greece	—	0.0	—	20.2	55.7	1.5
Ireland	—	0.0	—	27.1	72.7	2.1
Italy	59.9	2.2	61.6	23.6	59.2	2.3
Netherlands	86.6	0.2	72.4	22.7	67.3	4.0
Portugal	80.8	0.1	—	19.0	52.0	1.3
Spain	72.7	1.9	69.0	28.1	72.1	1.9
Sweden	67.2	0.4	—	29.7	79.2	4.9
EC[f]	*72.4*	*1.7*	*61.1*	*24.6*	*73.6*	*3.5*
United States	95.4	—	—	—	92.8	—
Japan	41.3	—	—	—	90.8	—

Source: European Audiovisual Observatory, *Statistical Yearbook* 1998, 1999 (Strasbourg, France).
a. In percentage of total entrances.
b. In percentage of hours broadcasted (weighted by audience).
   Data for U.S. films are available only for 1996 (for comparison, data for U.S. fiction works for the same year are presented).
c. In percentage of households.
d. Expenditures in current euro per person.
e. The 1997 share is 8.7 percent if coproduced British-U.S. films are included as EC films.
f. EC simple averages of the columns (based on the 15 member states) are indicated by italics.

A newly emerging source of dissatisfaction in France is the role of subsidies. Until the very early 2000s, criticisms had been limited to the subsidy pattern, with certain observers finding the subsidy share granted to distribution to be excessive, with a notable exception in a weekly newspaper.[19] But sweeping criticism erupted unexpectedly with a hot debate between directors and film critics. In a paper published in one of the major French newspapers, certain directors bitterly accused film critics of "premeditated assassinations" and of wanting "to kill off all commercial French cinema designed for a mass audience."[20] The article generated an outcry, which leads to two key observations. First, directors producing small-budget cultural films did not endorse the stated accusations (as the quote shows, the article referred to "commercial" films), whereas directors specializing in "pure" entertainment movies did not intervene in the controversy. This clear split among directors of three types of films ("pure" entertainment, cultural, and "in-between") is crucial not only because it underlines that problems are concentrated in the "in-between" segment of the French production, but because, as argued above, it provides a basis for designing a worldwide acceptable subsidy regime. Second, the debate offered an opportunity for many commentators to criticize "a protection of film makers which has reached such a level that its beneficiaries are no more able to tolerate the least criticism,"[21] at last opening the door to criticisms of the existing subsidy scheme in the French press.[22]

Interestingly, doubts on the efficiency of the French subsidy scheme have very recently begun to emerge among official circles, as best illustrated by a very recent report from the French Senate.[23]

These criticisms have not reached the EC subsidy regime (as distinct from member states' subsidies), which is still widely perceived as beneficial despite the fact that the demand for European nondomestic films in each EC member state (for instance, the demand for EC non-French films in France) is not only small but also generally declined during the 1990s. This evolution suggests that the EC subsidy regime is self-destructing because CAPs constitute a barrier to an integrated EC film market, contrary to its stated objective. This is not surprising. National subsidies have artificially bolstered film production by "gluing"—the idea that investments are stuck in each member state, instead of looking to the best places in Europe—national investments in each member state. Rather than creating a demand for so-called "European" films, these "sticky" investments in a member state have been crowding out films from other EC member states. Ironically, the French film industry has suffered the largest crowding-out effect. In sharp contrast, the only EC film industry with growing market shares in the EC is the British industry, which has been characterized by a much lower level of subsidization for years (to a large extent, forcing it not to mimic U.S. films but to offer a British touch) and noticeable investments from the U.S. film industry in recent years.

TABLE 12
EC AUDIOVISUAL POLICIES: A BARRIER TO A EUROPEAN FILM MARKET

	Market share of films from:						Origin of first-time release feature films					
	Domestic	United States	Britain	France	Germany	Italy	Domestic	United States	Britain	France	Germany	Italy
	Britain (market share of gross box office)						**Britain**					
1992	6.8	90.6	—	1.0	0.1	0.0	11	59.9	—	6.6	0.9	0.9
1993	2.5	94.2	—	0.7	0.0	0.0	10.2	57.2	—	6.4	0.8	0.8
1994	8.8	90.2	—	0.5	0.0	0.0	15.8	58.9	—	5.4	1.3	2.0
1995	10.5	85.2	—	0.5	0.0	0.2	16.3	60.7	—	5.0	1.0	1.7
1996	12.8	81.7	—	0.5	0.0	0.2	18.7	59.8	—	6.6	0.6	0.6
1997	28.1	69.3	—	0.2	0.0	0.0	23.5	57.1	—	5.7	0.6	1.2
1998	14.2	83.7	—	0.2	0.0	0.0	20.5	53.4	—	5.9	1.1	0.0
1999	17.8	80.5	—	0.2	0.1	0.5	23.3	52.8	—	5.3	1.4	0.8
2000	21.4	75.3	—	0.3	0.0	0.0	21.4	51.9	—	6.0	0.5	0.8
	Italy (market share of gross box office)						**Italy**					
1992	24.4	59.4	6.1	4.5	0.2	—	26.1	47.8	7.1	6.6	2.3	—
1993	17.3	70.0	4.7	3.4	1.0	—	27.8	52.0	4.2	5.0	1.6	—
1994	23.7	61.1	6.7	3.2	1.8	—	27.5	50.0	5.2	5.5	1.4	—
1995	21.1	63.2	6.4	4.0	0.7	—	22.0	52.5	6.2	6.7	1.2	—
1996	24.9	59.7	5.9	2.5	0.1	—	26.6	48.9	8.3	6.5	0.8	—
1997	32.9	46.7	10.8	4.0	0.4	—	22.9	47.9	9.7	6.8	1.1	—
1998	24.7	63.8	7.4	2.2	0.2	—	24.0	47.8	8.9	8.1	1.6	—
1999	24.1	53.1	13.8	2.7	0.4	—	24.8	43.1	10.9	9.2	1.0	—
2000	17.5	69.6	3.3	5.8	1.1	—	20.1	45.6	—	—	—	—
	Spain (market share of gross box office)						**Spain**					
1992	9.3	77.1	3.9	4.0	2.6	1.2	11.3	53.5	6.6	8.8	1.6	6
1993	8.8	75.7	4.1	3.9	1.5	0.4	18.3	51.3	6.2	7.5	4.9	3.3
1994	7.1	72.3	8.7	3.2	2.3	0.3	12.8	52.8	8.7	6.1	9.0	2.0
1995	12.2	71.9	7.3	2.9	1.1	0.6	14.1	45.8	7.9	7.7	10.6	4.1
1996	9.3	78.2	5.8	2.7	0.4	1.6	17.7	39.5	5.2	6.7	5.2	1.9
1997	13.1	68.2	12.6	2.6	0.7	0.4	16.6	44.1	9.1	6.0	13.3	2.3
1998	11.9	78.5	5.8	0.9	0.5	0.3	13.0	47.9	8.0	5.4	13.2	1.8
1999	13.8	64.4	10.8	3.2	0.6	3.5	17.1	45.1	9.8	7.3	11.7	2.1
2000	10.0	81.6	3.7	1.6	0.8	0.2	—	—	—	—	—	—

TABLE 12 *(continued)*
EC AUDIOVISUAL POLICIES: A BARRIER TO A EUROPEAN FILM MARKET

	Market share of films from:						Origin of first-time release feature films					
	Domestic	United States	Britain	France	Germany	Italy	Domestic	United States	Britain	France	Germany	Italy
Germany (market share of gross box office)							**Germany**					
1992	9.5	82.8	2.5	2.7	—	0.2	21.9	45.1	7.3	8.7	—	4.2
1993	7.2	87.8	1.1	2.0	—	0.1	25.5	49.4	5.3	8.0	—	0.4
1994	10.1	81.6	4.8	1.5	—	0.1	22.8	50.2	6.8	7.2	—	1.1
1995	6.3	87.1	2.2	1.7	—	0.1	24.2	51.9	5.0	5.0	—	1.5
1996	15.3	75.1	7.0	1.0	—	0.1	22.3	52.3	4.9	6.3	—	1.0
1997	17.3	70.5	8.5	2.9	—	0.1	21.3	47.2	8.4	7.3	—	1.0
1998	8.1	85.4	5.2	0.7	—	0.3	16.9	56.9	6.4	5.4	—	2.4
1999	11.1	78.6	—	0.7	—	—	—	—	—	—	—	—
2000	9.4	81.9	—	0.9	—	—	—	—	—	—	—	—
France (market share of gross box office)							**France**					
1992	35.0	58.2	1.6	—	0.6	0.8	41.6	30.2	3.0	—	1.2	2.5
1993	35.1	57.1	2.7	—	0.3	0.2	38.9	34.1	3.8	—	2.5	1.8
1994	28.3	60.9	7.0	—	0.5	0.2	35.6	35.9	3.4	—	1.2	2.2
1995	35.2	53.9	6.5	—	1.1	0.1	36.3	35.0	4.5	—	2.5	2.0
1996	37.5	54.3	5.1	—	0.4	0.1	38.9	36.3	5.2	—	1.8	1.3
1997	34.5	52.2	8.9	—	0.2	0.2	38.3	36.8	6.3	—	1.5	3.3
1998	27.6	63.2	4.5	—	0.2	2.1	38.6	35.5	8.3	—	2.0	1.1
1999	32.4	53.9	8.7	—	0.6	0.9	39.8	34.1	5.3	—	1.5	2.1
2000	28.5	62.9	4.7	—	0.6	0.4	38.2	35.7	6.8	—	1.7	1.7
2001[a]	41.5	46.4	5.7	—	0.9	0.3	40.3	32.0	6.3	—	2.2	0.8

SOURCE: European Audiovisual Observatory, *Statistical Yearbook* 2001 (Strasbourg, France).
a. Provisional figures.

Regulatory Reforms and Liberalization: *Shakespeare in Love*

The above evidence leads to the conclusion that domestic regulatory reforms are much needed. Thus, this section looks at two issues: Why have almost no reforms been launched? What could be the desirable reforms?

Explaining Inertia: *Citizen Kane.* There are several explanations of why almost no reforms have been established. First, there is the sheer importance of the media for politicians. Media professionals (for example, film directors and actors) are, by definition, masters of public relations. Their skills make them particularly apt at exerting powerful pressures on governments, as illustrated in 1998 by a few European film directors, who were able to provide the "coup de grâce" to the OECD-based Multilateral Agreement on Investment (MAI), despite the fact that it was already clear that audiovisual services were excluded from the MAI coverage.[24] Because audiovisual services are an essential tool of the day-to-day relations between the "rulers" and the "people," government officials need the expertise of media professionals on a regular basis. This gives these producers much more influence than their economic weight would suggest. (Increases in audiovisual subsidies are significantly correlated with French major elections.)

Second is the much-entrenched belief that CAPs are necessary for creating "quality" movies. There is no evidence to support such a belief, as shown by the two (admittedly crude) indicators for French films. The first indicator is based on the TV audience. As stressed previously, the lightly subsidized French films produced before the 1980s attract, even nowadays (despite the handicap of many reruns), many more viewers during prime time TV hours than the heavily subsidized films produced during the 1980s and 1990s—such a difference in attractiveness is not observed for recent U.S. films. The second indicator assumes that the only people who can recognize the virtues of French cultural films are those who attend film festivals. If this assumption is correct, the French "share of awards" in the three major European film festivals (Berlin, Cannes, and Venice) seems a crude, but acceptable, indicator of the evolution of the quality of French films. This share has dramatically decreased from roughly 20 percent (1981–1986) to 8 percent (1987–1994 and 1995–2000), if one does not include the Cannes Festival. (Including Cannes confirms the decline during the two first periods, from 16 percent to 10 percent but shows an increase to 14 percent during the third period.) All this does not support a strong correlation between the CAPs and "quality" movies.

These results are not surprising for economists who regard changes in artistic quality as largely exogenous to public policies. They may even expect the CAPs to have a negative effect on quality for the following reasons. Broadcast quotas tend to induce TV firms to produce more domestic films only (or essentially) to increase the number of foreign films to be broadcast, making quality a marginal preoccupation. Subsidies change the trade-off between quantity and quality by anesthetizing filmmakers' risk assessment, as indirectly revealed by the much higher ratio of films to viewers in France compared with the United States (there are roughly 1.1 films produced per million annual viewers in France, compared with 0.4 films per million in the United States).

Third, the balkanization of EC audiovisual markets by the many quotas, subsidies, and monopolies (public and private) introduced by the CAPs has left EC audiovisual firms with two main strategic options. The first is to replicate the EC system in Central Europe by establishing additional monopolies—an option relatively easy to implement but with very low returns (because of the smallness of the available markets) and with the costs of increasingly hostile environments. (Why should Estonians be happy to grant monopoly rights and rents to French or German TV firms?) The alternative option is to become global (world) firms. However, that requires such large funds that it cannot be done alone by EC audiovisual firms (which are small and underfunded). Going global makes sense only for EC audiovisual firms that are part of much larger and diversified companies; however, this option is still very risky, as best illustrated by the integration of Universal Studios or even Canal Plus in Vivendi.

Last but not least, the absence of proposals for the liberalization of audiovisual services reflects the above-mentioned fact that audiovisual services companies do not know whether the existing policies make them net winners or losers, leaving no constituency for change.

Three Proposals: *Le fabuleux destin d'Amélie Poulain.* The three reforms discussed here are a preparatory step for multilateral negotiations and could improve the situation for both the entertainment- and culturally oriented audiovisual services sectors among WTO members. The reforms focus on the EC, but because all the suggestions are consistent with the letter and, more importantly, the spirit of the WTO, they also could be considered by other countries. Reforms should aim to eliminate the waste of European resources for making entertainment and to provide a much better environment for culture—a de facto, much neglected aspect in the existing CAPs.

The first proposal is to dismantle the CAPs quota regime. Justifying this action in a narrow WTO context—the highly discriminatory content of this regime—would miss the main reason of such an action: The existing quota regime is a crucial obstacle to a European integrated film market. As discussed previously, such quotas hurt every market participant, except the producers of bad domestic films. They create monopolies (hence inefficiencies) through price hikes or quantity restrictions, and as a result, they call for subsidies to be sustainable in the long run (at a large cost to public treasuries). The CAPs quota regime could be dismantled in three ways: merging domestic and other member state film categories into one ("European") category in the broadcast quotas, increasing the share of non-EC films in the broadcast quotas, and reducing the investment quotas (and eliminating the constraints of these quotas). The sequence of these measures should be examined carefully (ideally, the reduction of the distortions in the film markets per se should precede the reduction of the distortions in the investment domain in order to avoid the misallocation of investment resources in the most protected markets).

The second proposal is to make a distinction between subsidies for entertainment and subsidies for culture, eliminating the former and allowing the latter. Eliminating quotas but keeping subsidies for all kinds of films (a policy often suggested in Europe) would be inappropriate. The previously mentioned French debate between directors and critics shows that entertainment films can survive without state subsidies, but cultural films cannot, and the ambiguous case of "in-between" movies is not a serious obstacle to this distinction because most of these films have little cultural content. At first glance, such a proposal seems drastic and to have little chance of succeeding in Europe. However, the situation is changing. Eroding monopoly rents within member states' markets (such as for Canal Plus) will inevitably undermine a large source of subsidies. Declining market shares of European films in European markets will force operators in the film market to recognize that subsidies generate barriers rather than create a single market.

Subsidies for cultural films do not raise any problem of principle about their compatibility with the rules of the WTO. The direct and indirect effects of such subsidies on film trade are minimal because such films tend to have limited audiences and are not a substitute for entertainment films. The source of subsidies does not seem to be a serious problem in the WTO framework. Funding through the general tax system (or a proxy for general tax, such as the British National Lottery, which may be seen as superior to funding through public budget because it is more transparent) is nondiscriminatory. Funding through a seat tax can be treated as (partially) equivalent to a tariff, which is an instrument easily negotiable in multilateral trade negotiations.

Such subsidies raise two problems of implementation. First is the instrument that will allow their introduction to the WTO framework. The solution seems to be a "reference paper" defining the conditions of competition in films, that is, allowing subsidies for cultural films and prohibiting them for other types of films. The second problem is to prevent filmmakers from improperly using subsidies for films other than cultural films. Such a problem is not serious in countries acting in good faith, because the distinction between entertainment and cultural films is easy to make and because cultural films rarely require large funds. For instance, French subsidies to cultural films amount (by all possible standards) to less than 30 percent of the total amount of public subsidies. But the problem does exist in the absence of good faith behavior by some WTO members. To monitor this risk, WTO member states should be requested to notify an agreed international body of their subsidies— perhaps an embarrassing exercise because it might reveal how amazingly little countries invest in their culture (and how culture is an excuse for sheer protectionism of narrow domestic economic interests).

The third proposal deals with the serious, and fundamentally domestic, issues raised by an efficient regime of subsidies for cultural films, that is, of an efficient "patronage." Such issues are completely ignored by the existing CAPs. To what extent can democratic institutions (that is, elected representatives and government officials) and associated bureaucracies (such as the French Centre National de la Cinématographie) be effective "patrons"? Being a patron implies the willingness to take risks and be ready to pay for the possible mistakes and corresponding losses. In democracies, representatives and government officials are intrinsically reluctant to take risks because they could be accused of favoritism. In addition, they never pay for their errors—the taxpayers do. Under these conditions, it is difficult for public authorities to promote culture directly (except in the narrow sense of preserving uncontroversial historical items and landmarks).

As a result, a serious treatment of culture in the film industry (as well as in other arts) requires adequate domestic regulations for art foundations and for innovative structures for patronage (for example, the British system of "franchised units"). Each country should make an in-depth examination of its capacity to provide the appropriate regulations and institutions for the support of its culture. These are purely domestic problems, and such regulations and institutions are unlikely to raise a problem with the WTO principle of nondiscrimination. In fact, a patron of French culture could be a U.S. institution or person (as in the late 1800s and early 1900s, with the U.S. tycoons and French Impressionists), and filmmakers producing movies nurtured by and enriching French culture could be natives of other countries.

In conclusion, none of these three proposals threatens "culture" or the WTO. To the contrary, they all offer opportunities to design better mechanisms for patronage than the defaulting ones on which the existing protectionist policies rely. The WTO is perfectly fitted for discussing the issue of culturally oriented subsidies (and other competition-related issues) in a reference paper specific to audiovisual services. There is no need to go to another international forum.

Postscript: And the Kiwis Came

The following postscript addresses four issues that emerged between the Uruguay and the Doha Rounds—during the late 1990s and early 2000s.

First, during the Uruguay Round, Hollywood was dominant in entertainment movies and fiction TV shows. Today, Hollywood retains its unique capacity to produce movies that are seen in cinemas all over the world—it is a major European preconception that Hollywood aims to produce only "American" movies. However, the situation has evolved in the fiction TV segment. The existence of a much larger number of European broadcasters has generated a strong demand for more differentiated programs based on more local content (local actors, scenery). Because skills for making fiction TV shows are easier to learn, and digitalization has made equipment less expensive, TV programs can target national audiences and still be profitable. To keep their previous positions, U.S. firms have had to make joint TV shows with non-U.S. firms.

Second, the costs of making Hollywood films in the United States have skyrocketed, inducing Hollywood filmmakers to shoot their movies outside U.S. territory. Requests for protecting audiovisual interests in the United States against "runaway productions" have emerged, as illustrated by a dispute between the United States and Canada over American movies being shot in Canada. What was at stake was (explicitly) "the small business that supports the film industry, . . . caterers, rental equipment business, electricians, etc."[25] and not, for example, the authors, directors, actors, and scriptwriters, that is, all the sources of culture.

Third, digitalization has created huge possibilities for creating images, including "virtual" images, at low cost. Countries that have not previously been involved in audiovisual production—but have workers who have digitalization skills and untapped natural resources—have been able to attract large productions, as best illustrated by *The Lord of the Rings*, which was mostly produced in New Zealand. (Interestingly, this movie is considered to be of U.S. origin in most countries, but of New Zealand origin by the French authorities.) As a result, competition between possible places to shoot films and fiction TV shows has tremendously increased.

Fourth, the strengthening of the Internet-based economy has dramatically changed the market prospects for cultural films. The Internet is a very cheap and widespread means of disseminating cultural films, which, by nature, tend to attract geographically dispersed audiences. Forces in the EC that want to extend to Internet-related audiovisual services the barriers and restrictions imposed on audiovisual services channeled by other means of communication are suicidal from the cultural point of view. In terms of the audiovisual services sector, the EC probably has more to gain from an untaxed and free Internet than the United States does.

Interestingly, all these issues challenge the U.S. comparative advantages in movies shown in cinemas—there is no such thing as producers with permanent advantages. As a result, they favor situations that can be seen by negotiators as more "balanced" between market operators in the United States, the EC, and elsewhere; hence, if more frequent and recognized, these evolving comparative advantages could make negotiations on audiovisual services at the WTO easier.

4

Conclusion

The audiovisual services sector in the Doha Round is significantly different from the audiovisual services sector of the Uruguay Round, in which negotiations focused primarily on film production, film distribution, and global broadcasting of audiovisual services. We come unanimously to the conclusion that new technologies and worldwide access to a multitude of entertainment and information services have stimulated the growth and development of audiovisual services and products from around the globe. Siwek proposes a proactive role in taking advantage of the global technological changes and suggests that the United States develop a reference paper that focuses on the distribution of audiovisual products over the Internet. Messerlin and Cocq optimistically outline the ongoing profound economic and technological changes in the large EC film markets.

Moreover, note that both Messerlin and Cocq stress the fact that only a limited group of WTO member states, including the United States, has taken substantial positive commitments at the various stages of audiovisual production, distribution, and transmission. Siwek emphasizes in this context that MFN exemptions to the GATS should be seen as temporary in nature contrary to the EU view, which characterizes its cultural exemption to MFN as "indefinite." Messerlin and Cocq stress the balkanization of EC audiovisual markets by the many quotas, subsidies, and monopolies (public and private) introduced by the CAPs. They make the point that "reforms should eliminate the waste of European resources for making entertainment and provide a much better environment for culture."

Countries have committed themselves to progressive liberalization negotiations under the GATS in all services sectors, including audiovisual services. The difficulty in achieving progress related to audiovisual services derives from the fact that the sector is unique and that the GATS mechanism may not be sufficient to address the specifics of this sector. To achieve progress in GATS negotiations, negotiators should reach an outcome that provides a mechanism to address different countries' concerns. The outcome of negotiations could result in a protocol that would establish rules for the use of subsidies, protect intellectual property rights, and contain provisions on how to protect culture by way of linkages with relevant cultural agreements.

Notes

Chapter 1: Introduction

1. United Nations Conference on Trade and Development (UNCTAD), *Provisional Agenda and Annotations,* TD/B/COM.1/EM/20/1 (New York: UNCTAD, August 14, 2002), 1.

2. Byung-il Choi, "Culture and Trade in the APEC. Case of Film Industry in Canada, Mexico and Korea," APEC Study Series 02-01 (Seoul: Korea Institute for International Economic Policy, October 2002).

3. As defined in the Services Sectoral Classification List. World Trade Organization, Note of the Secretariat, *Services Sectoral Classification List,* MTN.GNS/W/120 (Geneva: WTO, July 10, 1991).

4. World Trade Organization, Council for Trade in Services, Special Session, *Communication from the United States—Audiovisual and Related Services,* S/CSS/W/21 (Geneva: WTO, December 18, 2000).

5. The conclusions adopted by the General Affairs Council on October 26, 1999 form the negotiating mandate for the European Commission and are also valid for the negotiations on the built-in agenda. As far as audiovisual services are concerned, this mandate has also been confirmed for the Doha Development Agenda negotiations. "During the forthcoming WTO negotiations, the Union will ensure, as in the Uruguay Round, that the Community and its member states maintain the possibility to preserve and develop their capacity to define and implement their cultural and audiovisual policies for the purpose of preserving their cultural diversity." Council Resolution of January 21, 2002 on the development of the audiovisual services sector, *Official Journal of the EC,* 2002/C32/04, http://europa.eu.int/comm/avpolicy/extern/gats_en.htm.

6. UNCTAD, *Provisional Agenda,* 13.

7. World Trade Organization, Council for Trade in Services, Special Session, *Communication from Brazil—Audiovisual Services,* S/CSS/W99 (Geneva: WTO, July 9, 2001).

8. World Trade Organization, Council for Trade in Services, Special Session, *Communication from Switzerland—GATS 2000, Audiovisual Services,* S/CSS/W/74 (Geneva: WTO, May 4, 2001).

9. U.S. International Trade Commission, *General Agreement on Trade in Services: Examination of Major Trading Partners' Schedules of Commitments* (USITC Publication 2940, December 1995), 46–47.

10. Organisation for Economic Co-Operation and Development, "Policy and Regulatory Issues for Network-Based Content Services," DSTI/ICCP/IE(96) 9/REV1 (Paris: OECD, August 4, 1997), 6.

11. Jeanne S. Holden, United States Information Agency staff writer, *Global Film Trade, Cultural Goals Compatible* (United States Information Agency, April 1996), available at http://usinfo.state.gov/journals/ites/0496/ijee/ej17.htm.

Chapter 2: Changing Course
Stephen E. Siwek

1. "United States and European Union Reach Agreement on Global Electronic Commerce," *Business America* 119, no. 1 (January 1998): 7–8, available at http://www.technology.gov/digeconomy/20.htm.

2. Several restrictions on market access that are maintained by U.S. trading partners are identified subsequently in this paper. A comprehensive source of such restrictions can be found in "Trade Barriers to Exports of U.S. Filmed Entertainment," Report to the United States Trade Representative (Los Angeles: Motion Picture Association, December 1998).

3. World Trade Organization, "Guide to Reading the GATS Schedules of Specific Commitments and the Lists of Article II (MFN) Exemptions," 1, available at http://tsdb.wto.org/wto/JobNo2255.html.

4. Geza Feketekuty, "Principles of Sound Regulation in Services: The Key to Long Term Economic Growth in the New Global Economy," presented at the International Workshop on Trade in Services: China and the World (Beijing, December 8–9, 1998), 17, available at http://www.commercialdiplomacy.org/articles_news/china1.htm.

5. World Trade Organization, *Understanding the WTO*, 3rd ed. (World Trade Organization, September 2003), 33, available at http://www.wto.org/english/thewto_e/whatis_e/tif_e/understanding_e.pdf.

6. Masamichi Kono, "Liberalization of Services Trade Under the General Agreement on Trade in Services," presented at the International Workshop on Trade in Services: China and the World (Beijing, December 8–9, 1998), 6–7.

7. Ibid., 7.

8. In Japan, certain restrictions on foreign ownership of cable TV operations and DTH facilities have been the subject of negotiation under the U.S.-Japan Enhanced Initiative on Deregulation and Competition Policy. The Ministry of Posts and Telecommunications has announced that it will amend the broadcast law in the future.

9. Indeed, the EU's commitments in telecommunications specifically exclude broadcasting.

10. S. Wildman and S. Siwek, *International Trade in Films and Television Programs* (Cambridge, MA: American Enterprise Institute/Ballinger Publishing Company, 1988), 136.

11. "National Study of Trade in Services," (Washington, DC: Office of the U.S. Trade Representative, December 1983), 255.

12. See, for example, Patrick A. Messerlin and Emmanuel Cocq, "Preparing Negotiations in Services: EC Audiovisuals in the Millennium Round," presented at the World Services Congress 1999 (Atlanta, November 1–3, 1999), available at http://gem.sciences-po.fr/textes/ten/WSC99-000235.pdf.

13. Under Article V of the GATS, member states can enter into regional agreements in order to further the process of economic integration among the countries concerned. Proponents of MFN exemptions in audiovisual services may claim that such culturally based discrimination is needed to further goals of economic integration.

14. World Trade Organization, "European Communities and Their Member States: Final List of Article II (MFN) Exemptions," *General Agreement on Trade in Services*, GATS/EL/31, April 15, 1994, 1–3.

15. The GATS agreements on market access in basic telecommunications services are one of the most significant accomplishments of the GATS negotiations.

16. The U.S. list of MFN exemptions also specifies differential treatment of tax deductions for expenses of an advertisement carried by a foreign broadcast and directed primarily at the U.S. market only when the broadcast undertaking is located in a foreign country that allows a similar deduction for an advertisement placed with a U.S. broadcast undertaking.

17. "Significance of Global Telecom Deal Lies in the Small Print," *Telecom Markets*, no. 310 (February 27, 1997): 9.

18. "French New Multiplex Projects Multiply," *Screen Digest*, June 1999, 122.

19. Robert Marich, "Movie Theaters Gaining Ground," *Los Angeles Times*, February 18, 1999, 6.

20. Ibid.

21. "Trade Barriers to Exports of Filmed Entertainment," 1999 Report to the United States Trade Representative (Los Angeles: Motion Picture Association, 1999), 258.

22. Ibid., 22.

23. Ibid., 257.

24. Ibid., 253.

25. Ibid., 6.

26. Ibid., 255.

27. Alan Forrest, "Can Community Support Measures Have a Decisive Impact on European Film and Television Production?" *European Business Journal* 8, no. 1 (1996): 36–48.

28. Ibid.

29. Ibid.

30. European Community, Council Directive 89/552/EEC (October 3, 1989), amended by Directive 97/36/EC (Brussels, June 30, 1997), 3.

31. World Trade Organization, *Understanding the WTO*, 3rd ed. (World Trade Organization, September 2003), 34, available at http://www.wto.org/english/thewto_e/whatis_e/tif_e/understanding_e.pdf.

32. See Messerlin and Cocq, "Preparing Negotiations," for a comprehensive analysis of net winners and losers under the European CAPs.

33. Anonymous, "United States and European Union Reach Agreement on Global Electronic Commerce," *Business America* 119, no. 1 (January 1998): 7–8, available at http://www.technology.gov/digeconomy/20.htm.

34. Ibid.

35. Bruce M. Owen, *The Internet Challenge to Television* (Cambridge, MA: Harvard University Press, 1999), 151.

36. "United States and European Union Reach Agreement on Global Electronic Commerce," *Business America* 119, no. 1 (January 1998): 7–8, available at http://www.technology.gov/digeconomy/20.htm.

37. "News Digest," *Interactive Content*, September 1, 1997.

38. "Gigabytes Behind," *The Washington Post*, January 15, 2000, A22.

39. Owen, *The Internet Challenge*, 234.

40. Ibid., 233.

41. Anonymous, "Electronic Commerce Heads for the World Trade Organization," *Business America* 119, no. 1 (January 1998): 24.

Chapter 3: Preparing Negotiations in Services
Patrick A. Messerlin and Emmanuel Cocq

1. World Trade Organization, *Audiovisual Services*, Background Note by the Secretariat S/C/W/40 (Geneva: WTO, 1998).

2. This is the title of a $3 million, forty-minute film made specifically for initial Internet distribution by Metafilmics. Andrew Pollack, "New Cinema Frontier: Premiere Will Be on Internet," *International Herald Tribune*, August 25, 1999, 1.

3. Details about French specifics can be found in Patrick A. Messerlin, *European Film Policy: "La Grande Illusion"* (London: Centre for Policy Studies, 1997); Emmanuel Cocq, *Analyse économique de la politique cinématographique française* (Paris: Institut d'Etudes Politiques de Paris, 2000).

4. European Community, Directive 97/36/EC, Chapter III, article 4 (Brussels, 1997).

5. Bradley W. Stetser, *L'économie politique des quotas de diffusion* (Paris: Institut d'Etudes Politiques, 1996). In Britain, BBC channels broadcast few American movies but BSkyB broadcasts such films almost exclusively, whereas *every* French TV channel broadcasts at most 40 percent of American movies, so it can be argued that a British viewer equipped with satellite TV still has a less-restricted choice at any time of the day than a French viewer. But also note that a French viewer buys twice more blank videocassettes than his or her British

counterpart, probably for reasons not unrelated to the dispersion and relative scarcity of U.S. films over channels.

6. Quotas can be defined on a firm-by-firm basis. For instance, Canal Plus can broadcast 364 movies, whereas the other French air-TV channels can broadcast only from 170 to 192 films per year. Canal Plus is not subjected to "global" quotas on broadcasting movies during prime time hours (the other air-TV channels can broadcast only 104 films during these hours).

7. This market share dropped to 46 percent in 2001, a very exceptional year for French movies.

8. A "guide" of no less than 318 pages lists 17 main types of subsidies (excluding regional aids). Jean-Pierre Fougea, Anne Kalck, and Pascal Rogard, *Les aides au financement* (Paris: Editions Dixit, 1993). In a nutshell, French film subsidies can be divided into aids to production (automatic or selective) and to cinemas. A specificity of French subsidies (see table 9) is the large share granted to cinemas ("exploitation" in French legal jargon) compared with aids to production. Cinemas are said to be necessary for showing new films and generating cultural diversity. However, this official rationale does not fit reality: Twenty percent of French films produced never reach cinemas, and many films are shown for only a few days. Another rationale for large subsidies to cinemas is that 20 percent of the French cinemas (representing roughly 50 percent of the number of French viewers in cinemas) are owned by the three major French studios (Gaumont, Pathé, and UGC).

9. Cocq, *Analyse économique*.

10. A last source of subsidies consists of subsidies paid to factors of production of films. Until two years ago, the unemployment benefits for actors and other film workers had been extraordinarily generous (even by French standards) and extraordinarily inequitable (benefits were proportional to wages and fees).

11. Since 1997, Canal Plus has had a competitor, a joint venture (TPS) of all the major French air-TV channels, France Telecom, and Lyonnaise des Eaux (a utility company, and Vivendi archrival). However, Canal Plus remains dominant, with 4.5 million subscribers in late 2001, compared with 1.1 million subscribers for TPS. However, the rent-erosion process has started.

12. Messerlin, *European Film Policy*.

13. "Le Journal d'Anne Frank, dessin animé japonais, est devenu français," *Le Monde*, February 24, 2000.

14. "Le CNC n'a pas les moyens de refuser les aides au film de Jean-Pierre Jeunet," interview with David Kessler, Managing Director of the CNC, *Le Monde*, October 22, 2003, 32.

15. A precise comparison between countries and over time is difficult because there is no definition of what constitutes film production. Some TV works or documentaries are taken into account by some member states (e.g., Germany and Italy, and France since 1999).

16. J. E. de Cockborne, Reuters News Service, March 10, 1999.

17. This series of interviews has been published in the newspaper *Libération*, October 26–30, 1999.

18. For instance, see "Vers la fin de l'exception française?" *Le Monde*, January 11, 2000. It remains to be seen whether the exceptionally high share of French films in 2001 may reverse this declining support. So far, it is not the case (and to our point of view, it will never be the case).

19. "L'Académie française, cette calamité," *Marianne*, August 30, 1999, 57–61.

20. Later on, one director even suggested that "no negative review of a film be published before the weekend that follows its cinema release"—a fascinating extension of the quota regime to critics ("Les cinéastes français se réunissent pour discuter du rôle de la critique," *Le Monde*, November 4, 1999, 35; "Nous, cinéastes," *Libération*, November 25, 1999, 33).

21. "Une certaine idée du cinéma," *Le Monde*, December 16, 1999, 1.

22. "Cinéma: la machine à faire des flops," *Capital*, February 2000, 90–92.

23. Yves Gaillard and Pierre Loridant, "Revoir la règle du jeu: mieux évaluer l'efficacité des aides publiques au cinéma," Rapport d'information du Sénat no. 276, *Les Rapports du Sénat* (Paris, 2003).

24. David Henderson, *The Multilateral Agreement on Investment Affair: A Story and its Lessons* (London: Royal Institute for International Affairs; Paris: Groupe d'Economie Mondiale, 1999).

25. Statement of U.S. Representative J. Weller, "Testimony before the Sub-Committee on Trade of the House Committee on Ways and Means, Hearings on the U.S. Negotiating Objectives for the WTO Seattle Ministerial Meeting," reported by *Inside U.S. Trade*, August 5, 1999.

About the Authors

Patrick A. Messerlin is professor of economics at Sciences Po, and Director of Groupe d'Economie Mondiale de Sciences Po (GEM). He has published extensively on trade policy, in particular on WTO matters and European commercial policy. After having been special advisor to Mike Moore, Director General of the WTO, he is currently cochairman of the Task Force on Trade and Development of the UN Millennium Project with Ernesto Zedillo, Director of the Yale Center on the Study of Globalization.

Stephen E. Siwek is a Principal with Economists Incorporated, an economic research and consulting firm in Washington, D.C. He writes and consults on international trade issues in motion pictures, television programs, and computer software. Mr. Siwek is coauthor (with Steven S. Wildman) of *International Trade in Films and Television Programs* (AEI Press, 1988) and coauthor (with Harold Furchtgott-Roth) of *International Trade in Computer Software* (Quorum Books, 1993). Since 1990, Mr. Siwek has also published studies on behalf of the International Intellectual Property Alliance that document the economic importance of the U.S. industries that depend on copyright protection. The most recent of these studies is entitled *Copyright Industries in the U.S. Economy: The 2000 Report*.

Emmanuel Cocq is a Research Fellow at Groupe d'Economie Mondiale de Sciences Po. He received his PhD in economics at Sciences Po in Paris. His research interests cover the liberalization in services and regulatory reforms in France, with a special interest in the audiovisual sector. He teaches the economics of the audiovisual sector in the doctoral program of Sciences Po.